Everyday Magic

Thorsons books by the same author:
A Witch Alone

Everyday Magic

Bring the Power of Positive Magic into your Life

Marian Green

Thorsons

An Imprint of HarperCollinsPublishers

DEDICATION
To all members of the Hawkwood Survivors' Club
who now lead the work and teaching in the
Western Mystery Tradition.
Bristol, June 1994

Thorsons
An Imprint of HarperCollins*Publishers*
77–85 Fulham Palace Road
Hammersmith, London W6 8JB
1160 Battery Street
San Francisco, California 94111–1213

Published by Thorsons 1995
10 9 8 7 6 5 4 3 2 1

A catalogue record for this book
is available from the British Library

ISBN 1 85538 438 8

Printed in Great Britain by
HarperCollinsManufacturing Glasgow

Contents

Introduction 1

Introduction

'...I would like to begin by presenting magick as "The art of influencing material events by essentially non-material means".'

Tony Willis, *Magick and the Tarot*

'Magic' is a very powerful and evocative word, bringing to most people's minds the twin concepts of conjuring and ancient mysteries. This book aims to show that the real, ancient arts of magic, which do not involve sleight of hand, deception or mirrors, can be brought into our lives today, to bring a number of benefits. Today, we have the language of psychology, the technology of computers and the physics of sub-atomic particles, the building blocks of all creation, but we still have the arts of magic, the crafts of talismans and the power to change our lives.

Like any other skill, the many and varied techniques of magic can be mastered by anyone with a bit of patience and the enquiring mind which seeks to go beyond the trite explanation of the way things are. Most of these skills involve the mind, the memory and the common sense of the practitioner. They are quite safe, for the forces which wield the powers to change our lives are parts of our own inner being, hidden and overlooked, but potent when called into action. Combining the ability to analyse the situation we find ourselves in with the practised arts which can make changes for the better, we will learn how to heal ourselves and those around us; we will develop patience and concentration and accept every opportunity which comes our way. We will become observant and be able to see into the future because we will see clearly what is in our daily vision. We can enter our dreams, and change that 'virtual reality' within our sleeping minds into actual reality in the world around us. Using ancient arts of ritual action it is possible to draw towards ourselves, with the power of a great magnet, all the things which we truly desire by being open to that power.

The arts of magic can be learned in the same way any other skill is learned, by patient application of study combined with practical effort. Results can appear miraculously and instantly once the basic techniques have been thoroughly mastered. Consider the effort required to play a musical instrument well. It takes regular practice of unexciting exercises for quite a long time before the finger movements, the rhythm and the quality of the music can be produced. Magic is the same. There are some everyday exercises to be performed, but they should be fun and be rewarding as you sense your skills increasing. There are aspects of reading, study and work which take time to perform properly, but the end results can be terrific. Only you, the would-be magician, set the limits. The more time, effort and regular work you put in, the greater the changes you will be able to make to improve your life and those of the people you love.

It is never too early nor too late to begin learning the basic arts of magic in the Western Tradition. The first skills are those of the mind, involving concentration, observation and relaxation. To be able to see the angels, the old gods and goddesses, the visions in a crystal ball or the future of your ambitions in the cards, you need to be able to make controlled changes in your level of perception, so that you can see beyond the pattern of the world which surrounds you to those realms beyond, where images of the possible futures lie hid and where dreams can be helped to come true.

Take your time, trying out the exercises in this book and others recommended in these pages. All this work is written about by adepts of today, working secretly in the world and achieving the kind of results of which you may be hoping for in your heart of hearts. Anyone can rise to great heights in modern magic, if willing to put in the necessary effort, just as anyone could excel at sport, music, art or business. (To avoid gender bias I have used 'she' throughout, but this applies equally to male/female.) Magic holds the keys to all fields of life and, properly used, can bring about marvellous results. All you need to do is to make a positive statement, 'I will try!' and you will have begun.

Chapter One
Magic in the Modern World

'Magicians are ordinary people, too, and have ordinary lives, jobs and families. While they may be aware of other laws operative within these ordinary lives, they never engage in the kind of role playing games described in occult pulp fiction.'

John Matthews, *The Western Way*

We are living at the end of the second millennium and yet the arts of magic, the lure of the occult and the fascination of ancient mysteries are still with us. Science has explained many of the forces of the universe, from creation itself to the shape and size of the myriads of galaxies, yet it still has many problems to solve. There are ways of splitting atoms and examining the smallest known pieces of creation; from the greatest to the least, science is probing for answers and yet certain patterns emerge. From ancient times thinkers considered that everything was made up of the Four Elements, Earth, Water, Air and Fire. Many creation legends are based on a Divine Mother, Father and Child. Here we have the numbers four and three. In the latest theories about the nature of all substances, these same numbers occur time and time again – fours and threes and twos, pairs which combine to make a third. From the latest scientific discoveries to the oldest legends, the same concepts can be found.

4

Magic relies upon similar sets of basic building blocks, particularly the Four Elements, Earth, Water, Fire and Air. These are not necessarily seen as just 'things', but as concepts, as abbreviated symbols for a very complex system. Actual pieces of rock for Earth, spring water for Water and so on may be used in ritual, both ancient and modern, because it is far easier to imagine the power of the oceans if we have a sample of it in front of us, but *real magic* is performed inside our minds, by focusing our intent upon a desired result. It is towards learning the techniques of control and focus of our consciousness that the many exercises used in magical training are directed. By working with a talisman, for example, a charged symbol we have designed and made for a particular purpose, we can focus the laser beam of directed consciousness on the objective, and, as time passes, bring it into being.

Modern magicians – and there are a growing number of adepts about – learn some of their arts under the tutelage of schools or colleges of magic, gaining expertise under the watchful eye of teachers, and some by book work. It is necessary to grasp the practical skills, which may involve the physical preparation of sacred objects, making a special robe or kaftan for rituals and even construction of an inner temple with all its furnishings, as well as developing the inward-turned states of consciousness. For those of you who are beginning your journey into the occult, it is likely that books will be your first companions, teachers and advisers. This is not an easy path to follow, because you may be lonely and fearful of trying out the practical exercises which prove to you the reality of magic. As a writer of text books on magic and as a practical teacher for over 30 years, I can assure you that most exercises taken from books written in the last 10 years should be safe if you apply common sense. They will not be productive, though, unless you are prepared to put some work into making headway on your own.

Some people are convinced that it is necessary to *believe* various strange things before you can take up magical work, but this is not true. Magic, like music, is an art which relies on experience, not belief. You don't have to *believe* you can play the violin, you simply have to have the practical experience of playing it. To be an effective magician you need to keep an open mind, neither swallowing wholesale the stories in works of fiction, nor denying the possibility of a spell working just because it initially seems unlikely. Gradually, as you go along, your own experiences will help you to be certain about the truths of the reality of magic because you will have seen them and felt them for yourself.

There is a lot of work involved, but so there is in any field of human endeavour which is worth striving for. You have to learn that the harder you work, the deeper you study, the more profound and rewarding your efforts will be.

One of the first things to be aware of is that you are not alone in your interest in magic or the occult. There are thousands of people from all walks of life out there, studying, working spells, performing rituals and joining study groups or magical lodges. Only when you recognize that, like you, others are reading this book, and they too are nervous, wondering what might happen if they dare to try anything out, will you feel less lonely. You should be aware of one of the oldest magical mottoes, 'To Know, to Dare, to Will and to Keep Silent', for this sums up the philosophy of magic, ancient and modern.

'To Know' is the first stage, perhaps the one you are at. The problem is: What is it you should know? You should know that magic is a reality as much now as it was when the first shaman served her tribe by finding water and food. In ancient times success in the unseen skills was vital, life-saving, and was entrusted to special people, who proved they had the skills, either inherited or learned. It could matter in times of drought, if the clan was led to a dry waterhole instead of a fresh spring; it could mean life or death if the source of food proved empty. Today our needs and concerns are of a much smaller kind – we mostly have a home, some means of feeding ourselves, prospects of work and aims for our old age. We need to know what we desire and to know that we have to follow the law of the Temple of Eleusis:

'Know Thyself.' That is a task each of us needs to undertake for ourselves as the first lesson in magic.

'To Dare' is another arduous concept in the modern world. In everyday life we don't have to 'dare' much, yet we 'dare' to drive, be a passenger or walk on roads full of other drivers nearly every day even though we stand a fair chance of being involved in a car accident once in our lifetime. 'To Dare' in a magical sense means to reach into new areas of experience, to attempt things we have no previous experience of. Every magical act, every ritual, is a new experience, even for seasoned practitioners of many years' experience. To meditate for the first time requires daring. To speak a spell, which is bound to have some effect, if it is done with intent, will need daring. Acting in a daring way will reward you with a sense of achievement, as well as giving you the benefits from the results of the spell.

'To Will' is often the hardest concept to understand because now our will is seldom engaged in what we do. The most obvious way of explaining magical 'will' is in the sense of when, against someone else's advice, you say, 'I *will* go to the party!' You have made up your mind and no matter what the consequences of your actions might be, you are determined to proceed. In all areas of practical magic it is necessary to learn how to consult your True Will. This is not simply giving in to whims or pursuing the idea of the moment, but having a specific urge to act in a particular way. It takes a while to learn this concept, but it is essential because it is the directed will, combined with the focused consciousness, that makes magic work.

'To Keep Silent' might seem both obvious and puzzling in this age of open life. Silence has two meanings. One is to keep your mouth shut and not discuss your occult work or interest. That can be a valuable lesson to learn. If you don't tell any casual friend about what you are doing, you won't find your activities bandied about, scorned or laughed at. People can be very unkind about things they don't understand and it doesn't take much, if there is anyone around who wants to make trouble, for them to start accusing you of things you don't or wouldn't do, if they get wind of your interest in magic. Silence has a second aspect too. In today's world there is little real silence. We are bombarded with sounds all day long, wherever we are. Some of these sounds are of our own choosing – music or TV or a personal stereo to blot out sounds of traffic or other disturbance. Today to turn off the music, to close the window, to seek quiet, is a rare pursuit, yet in magical training, it is essential. Silence allows us to listen to the 'still, small voice' within, which has guided mystics and prophets, seekers and scientists, creative workers and musicians throughout history. To enter into silence is an important and effective activity. It is only when there is silence that relaxation of your mind can take place. This inner quiet leads to revelation and clear thinking. It can put you in touch with the old gods and goddesses, allow you to hear the voice of your Guardian Angel or your conscience, and bring peace.

Like many of the exercises which lead to magical mastery, studying these four simple principles in your own way can lay firm foundation stones to the edifice of occult knowledge. In idle moments think about them and quite quickly you will realize there is a lot more to their meaning than first occurs to you. Like the importance of the Elements of Earth, Water, Air and Fire, these are building blocks of ancient and powerful knowledge.

Although many of the modern techniques can be described in terms of psychology and contemporary language, they are the evolved results of thousands of years of secret work all through the western region of the Earth. Practices are based on the ancient divinatory skills which have roots stretching from Ireland, through Britain, into France, Germany and Spain, south to Italy and east as far as the Holy Land. In all these countries small groups of initiates and solo individuals have preserved the legends and myths of gods and heroes, of adventures and quests, which are the coded teachings of magical skills and sacred arts.

In every land there have always been researchers, scholars

and those who sought for hidden, or occult, knowledge. At first their special crafts were shared only with other members of their clan or family, taught by the older generations to the younger. Those with extra talents were encouraged to add their own discoveries to the inherited wisdom. Only methods or ideas which no longer worked were discarded. Through the age-old art of story-telling, something far more important than mere entertainment was gained, for through using their imagination, in the dark huts and round the fire, the hearers of the tales entered, in their mind's eye, the place of the story, and became part of it. Today this same art of magical story-telling and guided imagination is an essential part of the traditions of the West. By learning to completely assume the frame of mind in which images generated by the dreaming mind can be seen and even entered into, magical work, to heal, to see the future and to improve your life, can become a reality.

Because we are a society in which literacy is common, instead of having traditional teachers or clan instructors we now turn to books and magazines for information. Go into any bookshop these days and you will find shelves of books on 'New Age' ideas and self-improvement techniques. Although called 'New Age', most of the ideas put forward in the latter half of the twentieth century have been around for thousands of years, even written about, in hieroglyphs or ancient runes perhaps, but there to be read by the wise. Now new teachers are arising all the time, putting forth their versions of ancient wisdom, reinterpreted for the age in which we live. Some of these writers and teachers are wise indeed, having spent long years in the magical apprentice-ships of ritual, witchcraft or shamanism, gaining skills of mind and hand to match the knowledge of forgotten priesthoods. Others have been to a few weekend courses, joined evening classes in some arcane knowledge and then, putting word to paper, pronounced some very shady 'wisdom'!

To find knowledgeable instruction in magic, as in car driving or brain surgery, needs care and forethought. Many of the people who are starting their interest in practical magic are mature people and are capable of making sensible choices, but the occult is a wide and varied field of study, and there are a number of areas where care needs to be taken. What is essential to recognize is that magic is concerned with change. It will change your outlook on the world, it will deepen whatever religious feelings you may have, it will lead you down mental paths which will seem strange to those who do not share your interest. What concerns you may be the fate of the Earth, rather than the price of cornflakes, or the need for a park, not a supermarket, if Mother Nature's gifts appear more valuable than some people's profits or convenience. If you come to accept, as many modern magicians do, that reincarnation is a fact and that we all live life after life, then death may become less frightening. You may also recognize that tasks can be completed in the next life, mistakes paid for and old love affairs continued. To accept that some aspect of you could be immortal is a large step, and it can alter the way you go about your daily life and how you deal with other people.

Many aspects of magical work and knowledge will change your attitudes to situations and even the people around you. You may well come to realize how many people are forced to act out of fear – fear for their jobs, fear of those in authority, fear of what could happen to them if their little schemes were found out. This fear restricts their activities, clouds their judgement and in the end everyone ends up losing out. If you become more aware, through your magical experiences, you will be able to conquer these fears, because you will see the true situation.

Also, if you learn to see accurately into the future, you will be able to make more successful plans in all areas of your life. As you become more sensitive to the feelings of others, you will improve your relationships with those who deserve your love. You can learn to become lovable, and gain friends and partners who really suit you. This is not achieved by exerting any kind of pressure on others, but by realizing what potential you have for love and trust. That is a far greater magnet to a beloved than any amount of coercion, magical or material.

Another factor will be self-knowledge. Once you study your own life, motives and desires, you will begin to recognize patterns of success in the past, areas of frustration, and perhaps clues to a happier and more fulfilling future. Often it is necessary to examine your current situation from a new viewpoint, using the relaxed focus of meditation. This can be extremely effective in that it sets your mind free from the restraints of conditioning. For example, perhaps in your childhood you loved to draw and paint, but the only job offered was one in a factory. This artistic ability has been forgotten and overlooked for many years, but in meditation, you begin to see beautiful pictures you have painted, life-like portraits or stunning posters made from your works. This seems like a dream, but it is not impossible in our Western society to change direction in mid-life. You may be impelled, by this magical reawakening or old talents, to go to evening classes, or, as a mature student, attend a college to enhance your skill. It might be a struggle, but, like all areas in which you are in control, you will gain great rewards.

Some of the changes that magical study and practice may bring to your life may be harder to live with. What often happens is that you wish to spend time alone in silent meditation rather than going down to the pub, or you read books instead of keeping up with the programmes on TV, or you make new friends at lectures on Druidry or at Tarot card reading classes instead of through your previous hobbies. These new friends and companions may have very different outlooks from people you have spent time with before, and this may lead to conflict or debate. It is easy to find yourself scorned because you have taken an interest in strange-seeming ideas. If you are able to think back to your own old attitude to occult ideas, astrology or alternative healing, you may realize how your direction has changed. For those left behind in your leap towards personal knowledge and power, your interests and companions may appear very strange. You need to be aware of this, so that if people start to turn nasty when you mention that you have bought some Tarot cards or have enjoyed a book on practical witchcraft, you can explain that it is *your* life that is changing and not theirs.

The wide variety of subjects which may be seen as part of modern magic will, at first, appear confusing. The traditions of magic cover most of the world and all aspects of human endeavour. To begin with it may seem overwhelming to have to study ancient religions, the symbolism of the Four Elements and the history of your own land, together with the practical arts of meditation and inner journeying. There is no simple way to explain how big this 'jigsaw' of varied material is, but gradually you will see the picture emerging, as you find, for yourself, the connections between each area of knowledge. It is no good saying study just history, or philosophy, or religion, because all these concepts are intertwined like those complex Celtic knot patterns which decorate many New Age artefacts. You cannot stop the world to see only one facet, so you will need to be aware that the separate threads will eventually weave into a single coherent picture. It will be patience which can turn your groping explorations into the occult into instant and effective power.

What every student of magic should realize is that, old or young, rich or poor, educated or not, the powers you are able to gain through your studies correspond entirely to the amount of effort you are willing to put in. It is like developing a sporting ability. If you train hard and regularly, you will find that you can run faster and for longer or get on the ball more often. If you train only once in a while or frantically to try to make up time, you won't succeed. The arts of magic require the same kind of consistent dedication. No matter what you may read or hear, the power of magic stems from inside you. No one can give it to you or sell it to you, no one can empower your spells but yourself. However, you will need training from a good teacher, which is best of all, or from books written by living and experienced authors which you can fully understand.

The exercises shown in this work are designed to be taken in turn and tried until you get good and regular results – once is not enough! Each step will take you further along the path to magical mastery, but there are many different paths, many different traditions and types of magic which you might encounter. For this reason it is necessary to select a path which appeals to you and stick to it. It is the same in travelling – if you set out to reach one city then you need to follow the best route to that city, not take turnings at random or ignore signs which direct you to your goal. If in magic you start off following a Celtic path, for example, you can study the legends of the Holy Grail, the arts of the Druids and the magics of Merlin, King Arthur's mage, but you will need to ignore the runes and Norse/Viking or Saxon lore. To mix different traditions or sources of magic is as difficult and unpleasant as mixing foods from different kinds of meals. You wouldn't enjoy soup mixed with curried fish and custard on the same plate, would you? If you mix different systems of magic it is like mixing items from different courses of a lengthy meal. In the case of food, it would probably make you feel sick; in the case of magic, mixtures can make you feel very unsettled, disturb your sleep and cause you to sense conflict in your mind.

When you begin to study, but before you start to actually try out the various arts, it is well worth reading basic books about Natural Magic, the Qabalah (an ancient system of magic based around the symbolism of the Hebrew Tree of Life), Enochian invocations, Celtic mythology and Goddess worship. Today you will find many excellent short and explanatory books looking at the overall patterns of these varied traditions. Read these thoroughly and see which you feel most at home with. There are a few books which give examples from different nationalities of magic, including some rituals to try, but unless you understand at least a bit about the symbolism of the work you could end up confused and disappointed.

Take your time to consider the tales from each tradition, for these will appeal most deeply to your inner feelings. If, as many accept, you have lived before, it is possible that you were a Druid in a past life, or a medieval magician studying astrology and mathematics, an arcane art long ago. You might feel an affinity with Native American spirituality or mystical Christianity, or long for modern paganism. If you read widely, or, if the opportunity arises, are able to hear live talks about these different paths, better still if you can meet a practitioner and ask questions, you will soon find your steps directed to a school where you feel at home. Many modern teachers of magic operate through correspondence courses linked to personal meetings or weekend workshops. This gives you a chance to work at your own pace, but knowing there is a tutor who will help if you have questions. The workshops help you to find other people who share your interest and studies, so that you don't feel so isolated. You may also make new friends who certainly won't laugh and mock your magical aims.

If you search for good new books, the best ones will have lists of exercises which you can work on, so long as they are within your chosen tradition. You may also find references to probably the most helpful source of training, which are the many small specialist magazines, published all over the world. Some of these are simple broadsheet magazines run off at home by the editor, or they may be popular, glossy magazines freely available at a good newsagent's. The smaller ones are usually sent out only to subscribers, but most will send a sample copy for a small cost in stamps, if you want to try it. These varied journals nearly all contain details of study courses, both at public workshops or by post. A few short notes accompanied by stamped, self-addressed envelopes might put you in touch with exactly the teacher that you seek.

Here is a simple exercise to give you a feel of the work.

Silence and Stillness

Find a place where you won't annoy anyone else in your home, in or out of doors, and where you can turn off all sources of noise. Sit upright in a chair and close your eyes. (All exercises in Western magic are performed sitting in what is often referred to as 'the Pharaoh position', when your back is straight, your feet resting firmly on the floor or some old 'phone books so that your knees are comfortable and your hands resting on your thighs, with the fingers gently curled.)

First of all, just become aware of your breathing. Is it fast or slow? Deep or shallow? Do you feel relaxed and ready to try a simple test?

Feel the seat beneath you, the temperature of the air around you, the touch of your clothes, and begin to take very slow, deep breaths. Breathe out first gently but fully and then fill your lungs completely. If you smoke or have a breathing problem, take care and try not to cough or choke. Allow your entire concentration to be on this basic skill, breathing deeply out and then in.

Do this for a count at first of 10 breaths, and when you have tried it a few times over a couple of days, 20 breaths. Think how you feel at the beginning and how you feel afterwards. There should be a clear difference if you are concentrating wholly on the process. Ask yourself, when you have tried the 20 breaths a couple of times, 'What can I hear?' It may be your heartbeat, or the pulse in your neck, or the grumble of your tummy as you relax, or perhaps sounds outside still disturb your concentration. This is why quietness is so important at the start of your training. Unless you can maintain silence and concentrate for 20 deep, slow breaths without losing count, you will never be able to maintain the effort required for practical work.

To complete every day's session, take three deep breaths, then press your feet firmly on the ground, stand up and clap your hands, opening your eyes and feeling 'all there' but relaxed and calm.

It is necessary always to open and close sessions of magical work because in them you are more open, more 'psychic', and you don't want this sensitivity to spill over at other times. Remember, all magical work must be begun and ended, in more or less the same way, every time.

After you have succeeded at the 20 count breathing at least three times, you can go on to the next exercise.

Exercise Two

A Vision of a Safe Place

Sit still, close your eyes and allow yourself to relax completely. Breathe deeply for a few minutes until you feel calm and ready to begin.

Allow a picture of a place which you love very much to form inside your head. It could be a holiday scene, or somewhere from childhood, or just a kind of setting of countryside, cottage inglenooks or whatever makes you feel good. Revel in that vision, sense that it is a place of safety, a place of refuge from the troubles of the everyday world. See it in detail, feel the ambience, hear the sounds associated with it, and, above all, sense yourself as free and at peace. Build the feelings even if the picture is not yet clear.

Try this out as many times as you need to get all your senses awakened to this memory. Again, it is important that you can do this, because this aspect of memory is essential to all divination work.

Exercise Three

'Who Am I?'

Following on from the previous exercises, again relax and grow calm and quiet, then take yourself to your favourite place. Be sure you can feel with as many of your senses as possible, the scents, the touch, the sounds and the images of that favourite place.

Once you are truly there, in your mind's eye, allow yourself to think about the question 'Who am I?'

This may seem simple, and if you try these exercises lots of times, as you should, then you ought to get a variety of different answers. Your name is important, for you are a unique individual. There is no other person in the world with your skills, your memories, or all your potential for change and success. Become aware of this!

Also think of your roots, where your home is and has been. Who are your family, friends and those you love? How can you learn more about these relationships, both with place and with people?

Chapter Two
Gaining Positive Power

'We dull our appetite for life with negative words, and the words, gathering power with repetition, in turn create negative lives, for which our appetites become dulled.'
José Silva, *The Silva Mind Control of Mental Dynamics*

Negative thoughts and actions are the greatest barriers against success and, worse than that, they are totally under our own control. A very small change in our attitudes can bring amazing effects which astonish and delight us. Think about it! If you have always been told that you are useless, a failure, no good at anything, then you begin to accept those negative thoughts and you lose your ability to try anything new, even things which you feel you have done quite well before. The first lesson in magic is to learn that you can succeed at anything you want to do, so long as you are willing to make the proper effort for as long as it takes, using your time to fulfil that desire only.

Many people who hear about magic imagine that by waving a wand and muttering some words in a strange language, it is possible to conjure gold bars into being, or achieve success in romance, or become famous and rich. Common sense is sure to tell you that it can't be like that. You know that people who are rich and famous have become so because of their talents on the stage or in some other business. Some have inherited wealth, but again, if you read about their lives in the popular press, you will see that they have problems – their stately home is in need of expensive repair, they have difficulties ensuring the loyalty and silence of their staff, and other problems caused by being in the public eye beset them at every turn. Fame is not fun, riches bring both disappointments and responsibilities. You can aim for these lifestyles and magic can lead you towards them, but that would not guarantee happiness, love or honour from your friends and peers.

To achieve anything magical requires the application of True Will, as mentioned before. You need to be exact and precise as to what you want and to thoroughly explore all the implications of that desire. It is no good, for example, longing for a fast and expensive sports car if you can't drive very well, don't have anywhere safe to keep it, and couldn't afford the insurance and taxes! If your true desire is that car, then you can begin by gaining the driving skill, the secure garage and the money to pay for it by hard work and dedication. Magical spells can help focus your aims and though you may not get your car instantly, as fiction may suggest, you could win a competition for the car or discover a real bargain in a sale.

One person I knew wanted such a car and determined to get it by magic. He was not willing to work at getting his driving up to scratch, nor did he have much of an income or a garage! However, finding a ritual in a book, he performed the rite and waited, doing nothing. Nothing happened for some time, but his longing for the big fast car remained. One day the postman rang his doorbell and handed him a small parcel. It was not addressed to him, but the address was correct. Knowing there was no neighbour of the name on the package, he decided to open it, hoping perhaps there was a return address inside. Carefully he cut open the paper to expose a box and inside that, gleaming red, with smart leather trim and racing wheels, was an exact model of the car he desired. He had his car! The Inner Powers, who knew that he couldn't handle the real thing and had nowhere to keep it, have a great sense of humour, so he got the car suited to his taste. His magic had worked, but not how he might have hoped.

If you do seek to gain material objects, you need to be aware of the ethics of magic. You cannot have something which belongs to someone else, so if you hanker after the Mona Lisa, the best you might get is a good copy, or, if you desire someone else's partner, have another think! Objects that have owners cannot be won by magic because to get them is theft. Imagine you had a prized possession and another, expert magician decided she wanted it. Her spell works and you lose your special object. Unless you have the conscience of an angel, you would be furious and demand it back. If you saw it in the house of someone else you would go mad and try to take it back.

So magic cannot work like that. It cannot take actual objects from other people, either by direct theft or by taking them to pieces magically and transferring them to your home. In reality there are always spare items in the universe which have been thrown away, often after an owner has died, or which in some other way have become surplus to others' needs. So you can come by what you want without theft. It is always essential that you are absolutely specific that what you gain through magic has not been taken from anyone else.

You cannot and may not use magic to influence other people either. Again, in older books on occult work, there are spells to make people fall in or out of love. Please recognize that to use those kinds of spells, which make people act against their own free will or choice, is harmful. Such spells are harmful to the person whom you are trying to coerce and they are harmful to you, because you are bending the laws of truth, and that will cause an unpleasant backlash on yourself. Suppose someone fell in love with you, desired you, yearned for your company, day and night, and she had the power to will you to her side. She might well be someone you knew in your area, but whom you didn't like and certainly didn't love. Yet suddenly you would feel impelled to go to her. Your life would be most uncomfortable, being drawn to someone against your will, turning away from those you did love and acting very strangely. You would find your dreams haunted by the enchanter and her image would arise before you all the time. You would be bespelled and powerless. It is for that reason that acting upon anyone else is forbidden.

However, magic is not powerless to assist in matters of the heart. There is plenty of scope for using magic on yourself, to become the apple of your beloved's eye. You can use the power of magic to change yourself, to become lovable, adorable and desired. It could be hard work, it could take time, but there would be only blessing upon your efforts, not the distress and unhappiness that impulsion incurs.

Once again, you need to go back to the idea of positive thinking. If you go around saying to yourself, 'No one loves me, I am ugly, I will always be alone,' and so on, then you have sealed your fate. If you say, 'I may be lonely now, but soon I will find a friend/lover,' this puts a current of positive magic to work in your favour.

Spend some time, in your silent and calm meditation, considering how many negative thoughts affect your life. See how many times in that day you have said, 'I can't,' 'I won't,' 'It's too hard,' and so on. If you make the simple magical change to this attitude by deliberately saying, 'I will try,' 'I might be able to,' 'If I give it a go I might just succeed!', then you might just succeed! This may seem very small and not at all magical, but if you make the effort of taking a positive line, in all areas of your life, you will quickly be surprised at your success.

You will also need to look at the way others treat you. In all situations in life – work, family, job and love life – there are two sides, both willing the best for themselves. This leads to conflict of purpose, which, in the end, leads to misery and failure. Take each event as it happens and see, perhaps to begin with only in your mind, how a different approach might change things for the better, for both yourself and the others. Allow all kinds of unlikely answers to the mental questions you pose to float to the surface of your awareness, both the crazy and the helpful. Let them be considered equally, for it is often the unlikely approach which wins the day. If you always shout and argue when things aren't going your way, choose a day to become quite silent. You will have learned the value of this already, if you have tried out the earlier exercises. When you allow silence to reign, then other, deeper thoughts may surface, or in the outer world, beyond your mind, you may hear other voices giving good advice. Listen to others, even if you don't agree with them. Suddenly you may find that they start to listen to what you have to say. After all, wars are started by a breakdown of talking and usually end when talking starts again. Talking is one side of the equation, but listening is often the way to solve problems.

Be aware that there are always more solutions to any problem than initially appear to be available. Often a new factor needs to be introduced which will change (remember that magical concept?) stalemate into progress, be it on a national or individual front.

Time is another valuable asset in problem-solving. Try to ask for time to make changes; a minute or an hour or a month can mark the difference between a change for the better or worse. Magic requires time for any spell or ritual to work. Extra time allows you not only to think or meditate, but to still your mind and make it receptive to guidance.

Once you begin to see a way to put things right or improve them, using the experience you will gain by trying this attitude of positive thinking, you will be able to solve more and more problems. As soon as you are willing to say to yourself, or later, when you have more self-confidence, to the other people involved, 'I don't know what the solution is, *yet*, but we can find out!' or 'I haven't done this before, but I will *try!*', you may be astounded by the outcome. Always recognize the great thought that no matter what the problem or difficulty may be, somewhere in the universe, someone (most likely you) has the answer. Allow stillness of mind, meditation and openness to new ideas to guide you.

When you start to use magical methods in your everyday life

you will see that there can be a use for occult work on much larger projects. We all worry about the state of the world at large, the natural disasters, the illnesses which seem to be increasing all the time and the dangers of crime on the streets. Once again there are many practical ways in which we can add our dreams of peace, our desires for health and our hopes for safety to those of the millions of other folk world-wide who suffer the same fears. That is the strength. Even a few minutes each day used to send out positive thoughts multiplied by the minds of all the other aware human beings who share this little blue globe with us produces an enormous force for good.

To become effective at this art, which occupies so little of your time, requires imagination and concentration, as do all aspects of practical magic. Imagine as clearly as you can a place at war, for example. See the ruined houses that were once warm homes, see the burned-out wrecks of military machines, the scarred landscape and the frightened people, displaced and bereft of everything. You have seen this all on the TV news and in the papers, but allow it to appear inside your closed eyelids. Smell the smoke and the fear, see the shattered buildings and hope, sense the loss and despair, and then, as if by magic (for that is your power), begin to impose a new image upon the darkness. Look at the ground, muddy and pot-holed, and begin to see new green grass and little wild flowers growing there. Look at the houses and gradually impose a better view, with clear windows and bright curtains, gardens full of fruit and flowers. Look hard and see the faces of the little children light up with glee as they play at peace with new toys, and, last of all, discover the bright hope which burns in the hearts of all victims shining through their eyes as joy.

To get this to work will take a little time, but practise regularly every day. It only takes a few minutes and can be done while you wait for something else to happen. It is just a matter of direct focus on one particular tragedy, looked at over a few weeks. To see the ruins and gradually allow a better future to grow from the bomb craters takes time, but gradually you will be aware, as I am and others like me are, that new life and hope can gently emerge from the most devastated landscape. This is not easy, it costs time and effort, and the concentration you use may make you feel a bit weary, but the good it can do for total strangers is without price.

It should become part of your daily life that as well as using positive thinking to sort out your problems, you should spare a few moments of your time and effort to help those with infinitely worse lives. Magic has a cost. Because it causes changes, there is movement of energy. If you are selfish and only take, drawing on the power to benefit yourself, then, like a bank account full of money, gradually it will be exhausted. You will go broke and get into the red, arcanely, if not financially. If you make acts of kindness to a friend or stranger a part of your everyday magic, then the balance to your credit will remain stable or increase. You will find that the simple magic of a smile at a stranger may cause a ripple of good feeling across a whole city. One small act of kindness to another could repay you greatly, for there is bound to come a time when you need a bit of help. Perhaps your car has broken down in a strange place and you need a phone or a push, and a helpful person may well turn up, making you feel safe and offering assistance. We are all the children of the Earth, we are all linked by being made of the stuff of Earth, and so we are related to all people, all animals, plants, rocks and waters. Nothing is separate. It is this essential link which allows magical power to be passed from one person to another or to be stored ready for later use. Magic can act on you, it can act on people the other side of the world, and influences from the Sun or from distant stars can have a small (and usually unseen) effect upon us all.

Gradually, if you try out the first exercises in magical training, you will become more alert to what is going on around you. You may, at first, feel rather odd, for it is as if you have developed a sixth sense. Often it will be your dreams which show the first signs of change. Many people scarcely recall any details of the dreams all of us have every night, yet as you start to make room for mediation, positive thinking and silence, you will wake each morning with lingering fragments of your nocturnal adventures floating in your mind. Dreams are a natural window onto the hidden workings of your mind and memory, and many occult arts require you to be able to dream while wide awake and in control of the images. That comes with practice.

You may notice the attitudes of other people around you seem to change, some becoming more and others less friendly. What is changing, however, is not the outer world, but your own perceptions of it. You are becoming more sensitive to the actions and feelings of others. This can seem a frightening awareness, but gradually you will become used to it, just as you get used to new shoes, which may feel odd at first but become old friends in time. Everyone has far more levels of sensation than they are usually aware of. Like many magical activities, the sharpening of these senses and awareness generally will benefit you in the long run, but can seem weird to begin with. For example, when you start to understand the symbolism of any divination system, be it the Tarot, runes or palmistry, you will need those extra-sensory experiences to give a clear and exact reading. Perhaps you will also start to notice the atmospheres in your friends' houses or in places you visit on your travels. Some places may feel warm and homely, even if you are there for the first time, while others may feel cold, a chill which has nothing to do with the actual temperature.

In the streets your extra senses will tell you of danger, from a falling slate, perhaps, or unsafe footpaths. They might warn you of the approach of a thief so that you carefully lock your car. Becoming aware of even very ordinary things like changes in the weather will help you so that you take a macintosh because you *know* it will rain. That is the point. What you are gaining is an extra dimension to knowledge. We all know all sorts of things because we have been taught them or picked them up from circumstances, yet there are areas of experience which come direct as certainty.

This knowledge is also positive thinking, for it is the rightness of the idea or awareness which enters your mind directly, not through the usual channels of learning. Most people are aware of 'hunches' which may concern large or small events. Again, people often get this instant guidance from an inner level of their being in dreams or in those moments every day when unfocused attention wanders in a dreamy way. This is exactly the same sort of awareness which effective meditation brings about – open to new knowledge, yet uncritical and unjudgemental.

The positive and certain knowledge which comes from inside can often be surprising. Most people simply ignore hunches and suffer the consequences. How often have you heard folk say, 'I had a hunch that it would rain, but I thought better of it and didn't bring a mac, that is why I am now soaking wet!' It is as if there are two individuals vying for attention. One, the hunch, is right about the weather, or whatever, and two, the person's conscious mind, is wrong. Learn to trust hunches, for they are usually right and can be a source of help and a magical aid.

Although an interest in magic and occult matters is uncommon, it is an aspect of life which is shared by a large number of people in Britain, America and most countries of Western Europe. Traditionally, those who wished to practise the arts of magic and study the various traditions were members of one of the growing numbers of magical Orders. Although the names and locations of these Orders have always been a secret, known only to those who have been through the appropriate initiation ceremony, there have always been ways in which new students could make contact. For example, in the Middle Ages pamphlets about the work of groups like the Order of the Rosy Cross were circulated so that those interested could gain a glimpse of the work these hidden brethren were performing.

Traditionally quite small groups of initiates, numbering from about seven to perhaps 30 members, would gather to take part in the work of their magical lodge. A lodge was often a hall or part of a building specially made sacred for the work of the Order. It would be decorated in the style appropriate to the system of magic which the lodge performed. Many were designed to look like the great temples of ancient Egypt or the classical shrines of the Greek gods. Every part of the room contained images or symbols which helped to direct the participants' minds towards the aim of their work.

As novices, students would be taught some of the basic myths and methods of work, and when they were ready they would be guided through their first initiation, when the Mysteries, the secret knowledge of the lodge, would be shown to them. They would have to swear oaths of loyalty and secrecy, so that where and when meetings took place remained unknown to those out-side. They would probably take a magical name or motto which showed their aspirations, for example 'I strive for Good' or 'Peace is my Aim', often in Latin or Greek, and it would be the initials of this motto that they would be known by. As their personal knowledge and power grew, each candidate would be allowed to move up through the grades, like students in col-leges, taking on new information and new responsibilities at each stage. Those who won promotion would do so because of their abilities, as most magical groups would work on a system of meritocracy. In other words, those who were particularly good at divination or healing would receive further training in those areas, whereas others who excelled at ritual or making incense or robes or furniture would also have their place.

Today you won't find the names of these magical Orders in the telephone book, but you will certainly discover clues to the 'Outer Courts', the public training bodies, through which those who are keen enough and who hold the right attitudes will be taken in, in the Courses sections of the good occult magazines from the newsagent's. Today most would-be magicians start their training on a postal course, working through single lessons every month for at least a year or two. This is because the most important arts are those of the individual's mind. No one can learn the arts of patience and concentration for you, so which-ever way you intend to learn magic, at some point you will have to accept the discipline of regular daily meditation, exercises which strengthen your ability to visualize, analysing myths and

27

working with god forms. Now there are many good weekend workshops, too, which help students get a grip on the practical arts which are hard to get right from paper instructions. From these varied first steps those of you with the inclination to do the work will gain self-confidence and magical expertise.

To become an adept, a really competent magician and human being, takes a long time. Some lessons can be learned in hours, others may take months, but if you are really determined to succeed, there is nothing in the cosmos to stop you. Your skills will benefit the whole world, of which you could be a key part. Each of us is a player in the game of life and those who gain occult skills will be able to be more effective on their life path. There are no short cuts and you will often have to make hard decisions because you will have different calls on your time, and you must learn to act always with honour. It is no good taking over the most comfortable chair in the warmest room in the house and turfing your family out, just because you want to talk to angels! This will gain no help from the Inner Realms, who act at a very high level of ethics. The more you become aware of your own responsibilities to others, the more you act with care about their needs and feelings, the greater store of good you will be accruing in the Inner World Bank!

If you feel alone in your magical interests, especially if your family and ordinary friends think you are mad at best, and dangerous to know at worst, be assured that there are hundreds of people out there doing just as you are. They, too, are learning aspects of these ancient magical arts, some from books, some from practical schools and some lucky folk from individual teachers, both inner and outer. You need to trust your own feelings of rightness.

The various magical arts have been around in our world for thousands of years, and those who have studied them have often risen to positions of power and influence. Sciences, like chemistry and physics, arose out of alchemy, the art of the Black Land of Egypt, when early researchers tried to change metals into gold and raise the human spirit towards purity. They succeeded, for as well as the chemical experiments, an occult factor of Will was added and the end result produced very pure gold. Some may be seen in museums, for example the Natural History Museum geology room in London.

Your very first task is to try to define your own reasons and aims of working with magical power. Are you trying to have influence over people or are you wanting to be able to live more harmoniously with the world? Are you willing to help others or do you just want to get the best of everything for yourself? These motives are important, for, as I have said before, there are very strong ethical factors in play in all magical work and they are there to help those who work with the best motives. However, even that is not as simple as it seems. In some cases what seems right may have complicated long-term outcomes and it really is important to try to predict all the possible effects. Science tells us that 'Every action has an equal and opposite reaction' and this is as true in magic as it is in physics. This is another reason for taking time to think and plan before you use magic to influence events. A lack of thought beforehand can lead to troubles and disappointments later.

The following exercise is a way of teaching your body to relax whilst keeping your mind wide awake. Many people say that they fall asleep when they sit down to meditate or do other magical concentration exercises. This is usually because they are not concentrating on the work and reminding their inner minds of the subject or symbol of the meditation.

Exercise Four

Paint It Black for Relaxation

Sit upright in a firm but comfortable chair. You need to be able to keep your chin up so that it doesn't fall as you relax, and cut off your air and the blood supply to your brain (another reason why some people fall asleep!)

Gently close your eyes and imagine a large sheet of black

metal right in front of you. It is so big and so black that you can't see anything else. Then imagine a magical paintbrush covering the black surface with more black paint, which at first glistens but dries quickly blacker than ever. A deep matt black spreads all over. Work on this image until it is complete.

Once you have the black surface in front of you, absolutely matt black, you can use it as a screen to impose pictures upon.

See before you a great book with white and clean pages, and feel in your hand a beautiful pen. On the left-hand page of this book imagine yourself writing clearly all the things that are really good about you, all the things that since childhood you have *known* you are good at, all the aspects of your physical self you are pleased with, all the things you feel pleased about having achieved. Work at it, perhaps over several sessions. When you finish a session, firmly close the book, see the decoration of the cover and know that piece of work is completed.

When you have almost filled the left-hand page, begin on the right-hand page with things you don't like about yourself. Be honest, for no one will see what you have written. Fill that page with failures, might-have-beens. Again, take as long as you like, but at the end of the exercise each day firmly close the book and allow it to vanish back into inner space.

Exercise Five

I Have Done My Best!

This is an everyday exercise which should be done last thing at night and first thing in the morning, so try to make it a natural part of your going to bed and getting up. It requires just a moment to say, at the end of the day, 'I have done my best today, but tomorrow I will do even better at...' (If there is something you want to achieve, say that; if not, just add 'being me'!)

First thing in the morning, find time to say, 'Today I will succeed, I will strive to fill my need, because my magic is growing!' It is a silly little jingle you might think, but try it – it is magic!

Chapter Three
Creating a New Dream

'Dreams show us how to find a meaning in our lives, how to fulfil our own destiny, how to realise the greater potential within us.'

Marie Louise von Franz, *On Dreams and Death*

As you begin to awaken your inner senses by these first exercises in relaxation you may find your dreams change, to become more vivid and clear. You are learning to open a door to those regions of your inner self which can help and advise you. You may find humorous events happen and though you may see yourself in a strange setting, you find you can cope. Magicians who are successful are very aware of their dream lives and learn to achieve the same state while wide awake, in order to see the future and bring about healing. They live in ordinary homes, with jobs, friends and everyday commitments, yet all have become more effective through awakening their perceptions by both day and night. Such awareness helps them to be sympathetic towards the troubles of others.

Effective magic makes a person a good citizen, a kindly neighbour and a trusted friend. Because real occult work is hidden, no one trumpets abroad their connections with a magical Order or an ancient lodge. Those who seek publicity are the fakes, the show-offs, and really they know very little. What matters to serious magicians is the *work*, the rituals which

31

empower their magic and help individuals or whole countries towards a happier life. Right through history there have been secret bands of men and women who have used their powers of seeing into the future to predict, and perhaps shape, events. Today these hidden workers, both alone and in small groups, strive to bring about world peace, the end of hunger and justice for all. Though their aims are great and their work secret, every time the media shows a change of heart among the warring factions and the signing of treaties for harmony, these magicians will feel their efforts have been rewarded, and that their prayers and rituals may have played a beneficial part in the situation.

Of course not all modern magicians spend all their time working on Earth-changing events. Many work for healing, or to increase their own store of knowledge, or to reinterpret the ancient legends for the readers of today. Many teach, some publicity at open lectures or at study centres, while others train members of a particular society or Order. Always they are aiming to make the world a better place, or give effective power to heal or divine to their students. Much of their effort only affects those around them, but they become known in their home town as kind and reliable people.

You can join this hidden company of magicians if you want to. It will not cost you much money, though you might need to buy a few books, but it will take time, effort and personal commitment, just as it would if you wanted to play football in the Premier League or become a concert violinist. Each individual skill requires the same levels of effort, and if you decide that you want to become a true adept (and the world needs all it can get), then you will have to make some long-term plans.

You will have to decide which of the many options of magical tradition you wish to follow. There are perhaps 20 magical Orders in Britain, and hundreds in the USA. Each teaches a different sort of Western magic and the rituals, philosophy and practices vary from tradition to tradition. As I said before, like foods, they do not mix comfortably, so you will need to do some research and eventually choose a direction.

Making choices about things which are largely hidden is not easy in ordinary terms, but if you aspire to becoming a competent adept then you will realize that you may have other skills you can call upon. One very valuable process is to simply take pen and paper, and, in a quiet moment, begin to jot down the kinds of things which draw you to magic and which you feel, from your earlier reading or talks with friends, appeal most to you. Do you desire to wander round in brilliant robes in an incense-laden temple, chanting words of power and raising Elementals? If so, that gives you a list of techniques and activities to start with. You will need to sew and embroider your robes, discover how to blend the magical incenses from rare gums and herbs, build with your own hands the fittings and furniture of the temple, paint the symbols of the Four Elements, and master the ancient and sacred chants which empower the ritual. These are some of the steps, others will involve knowing how to construct a ritual and learning to enter the inner magical state of meditation to be able to receive divine guidance and help. Each small step is part of the way along a long and winding road, and every single step is equally important and valid.

You see, the magical arts are made up of many parts, some mental and internal, others very practical and ordinary. Without the balance of inner and outer, any magical work could be unstable and unsettling. As you try to decide which path you would like to take, you should be prepared to take some of the practical steps first. Even if you feel more mystically inclined, drawn towards the religious life, alone and self-centred, the same practical arts of meditation and the study of ancient texts and communion with whatever god or gods you choose will be necessary.

Examine your dreams, both waking and asleep. See whether any of them are pointing you in a particular direction. Are there myths and legends which have intrigued you since you were a child? Do the stories of King Arthur and his knights appeal to you, or Robin Hood and his life in the Greenwood? Each famous set of tales actually hides the rules of initiation into an ancient tradition. A magical way of looking at them is to imagine yourself as part of them, playing a minor character in these legends. See how a knight would go on the Quest for the Holy Grail, the archetypal symbol of healing and peace, in the world today. This is one of the schools of magic – modern people are still Grail Seekers, holding fast to the idea that somewhere there is a mighty object or symbol, which may not have a physical form, but which can be found and used to benefit the world.

For those who are drawn to the idea of the Wildwood, the way much of Europe was in ancient times, there are the stories of Robin, the Lord of the Forest, part hunter, part hero, defender of the poor and hopeless folk. With his companion, Marian, he lived in harmony with nature, using the bounty of the Earth Mother to live, to heal the sick and to bring hope in troubled times. Robin Goodfellow, the Green Man, bringer of spring and the power of returning life, was an archetypal nature god whose worship among pagans is growing. Natural Magic is an effective form of working, drawing on the powers of the Earth beneath our feet, the turning seasons of wonder and renewal, and the potent forces of the ever-changing Moon. Returning to our country roots can bring a great sense of homecoming, yet in today's world, it is hard for a town-dweller to live in harmony with country life. We endure the roar of city traffic, the hum of machinery and the yells of playing children, yet the sounds of farm animals and tractors, the early calls of cockerels, the whine of combine harvesters and other agricultural practices annoy us. What we can tolerate at home does not always transfer as tolerance in another place!

Some people are deeply drawn to the myths and legends of Ancient Egypt with its vast and beautiful stone temples reflected in the waters of the Nile. Even today the shattered remnants, eroded by the visits of millions of tourists, enthral and impel those who see them. Some learn to recall their earlier lives there, weaving the garlands, dancing before Isis and Osiris, the mighty ones in their shrines. In those stone walls, still showing the elegant and informative hieroglyphic inscriptions, there is wisdom, power and the energy of thousands of years of dedicated prayer, which modern magicians may draw upon in their contemporary rites.

To some people the power and beauty of Greece calls, and they hear Pan's pipes or see glorious Aphrodite enchanting their dreams. Again, there is a literary heritage of stories here: the great voyages of Ulysses and Jason, real journeys through an older world to seek fame or glory or treasure. The gods and goddesses are well defined, clearly painted in red on black pottery, their stories shown, their symbolism easy to read. We have a vast store of tales from which we can work back to the Mysteries, the sacred dramas with symbols only initiates could understand. All the ancient Mysteries still exist – they may seem hidden, but if we are drawn to follow a particular path, we will be shown ways in which we will be able to reawaken this forgotten knowledge. Nothing is lost!

Whichever path you choose to follow to begin with will only be a starting-point. But as you make progress, as you surely will if you try, then you will begin to see more clearly where you want to go, magically. However, unless you really do feel impelled to try a particular tradition, you won't want to start at all! Magic relies on the engagement of the emotions. You have to long to make a difference, to deeply yearn to change the world. A simple 'Oh, well, it could be fun' attitude won't get you very far. Magic *is* fun, it is rewarding and it can bring a kind of friendship only found in other close-knit clubs or families, but to empower your magic you need to feel committed and to want with all your heart to succeed.

When you share a ritual with companions there is a sense of unity and closeness which is very hard to describe. There is an old saying that you should meet: 'In perfect love and in perfect trust'. This is very true. Unless you love the work and the aims of your group you will have little care to add to the power and so their spells will fail. Unless you trust those you meet on the magical paths, whether teachers, companions, leaders or juniors, you will be unable to trust yourself or the unseen, inner guides you will encounter in meditation and ritual. The stronger the bonds of friendship and trust are among all levels of beings, the greater the forces they are able to handle collectively.

The trust and companionship you should gain within a lodge should flow over into the world around you. Gradually, as you discover your own worth and growing abilities, you will find you honour and respect all sorts of ordinary people you meet in your daily round. It is self-limitation or fear which prevents everyone reaching their potential. An early lesson of all occultists is to honour their own individuality, delight in the powers that they have still to discover within themselves and the things they will be able to do. Perhaps you lack confidence and are afraid of what magic really can do. But if you are daring and try even the most simple of these exercises you will see that you can become confident and strong.

A very easy exercise which you can try today is, when faced with something you are not sure you can do or a task you really dislike, to say 'I can and I will!' Make it a silent statement, if you prefer, but say it all the same! Take something like washing up – hardly anyone likes doing it, but if you see it as a kind of challenge, you may be able to find a way of doing it faster and better. A few moments deciding how you stack the plates, learning to use the running hot water to rinse glasses and eating utensils can save time. Soaking things whilst you meditate for 10 minutes might help with the pots and pans. Apply magical thinking to every dull task. Ask yourself, 'How would the magician Merlin tackle this?' (The answer is not to imagine he would call up a genie to do it for him, either!)

Exercise Six

New Ways with Old Chores

Once again perform the deep, slow breathing in and out for at least two minutes, until you feel calm and open to the deeper levels of your own awareness. Let your mind become ready to look at what you have to do which doesn't please you. Imagine yourself doing the chore in a different way. One magical way is to say to yourself that it is your True Will that you do the job extremely well, that you will get a sense of satisfaction from doing it. Perhaps it will occur to you that there is another way of approaching the work which would make it fun, or at least help you to get through it both well and quickly.

If you spend at least 10 minutes a day on this exercise for a couple of weeks, you may well be amazed at how, given a little peace and quiet, your mind can show you far more rewarding ways of doing things. If you succeed and really get the new method to work, you may gain praise for your efforts or be able to help others around you enjoy or improve their tasks too.

Like much of magic, this is not easy. You may need to really work at opening up and allowing your mind to reinform you before you see results, but the more you relax and let go, the faster results will come. They really will!

You can apply positive thinking to difficult events too. If you have to face an interview with your boss, imagine yourself, for a few days beforehand, as one of the heroes of your magical path. Think how that character would deal with a real adversary that he or she has to outwit. Not all problems can be solved by bashing or zapping enemies, as you will know from your own experience, so use practical positive thinking and find a way to come out of the interview feeling that you have done your best. Even that feeling can prove to you that you are better than you thought. Don't forget that real heroes are usually kind and considerate while still striving for their own side. It is the Pure and Gentle Knight image rather than the Berserk Viking that you should attempt to follow!

Although the various traditions of magic vary in detail, there are a few concepts which most of them share. One of the most important for any student to understand is the importance of the Four Elements. Symbols of Earth, Water, Fire and Air are often used to make sacred and set apart the magical circle, both for a solo individual seeking deep meditation and for the group or lodge, sealing their inner temple. Not only do these Four Elements traditionally give us the four magical instruments or weapons, but they are reflected on the cards of that primary divination system, the Tarot, as the devices on the four suites. The four magical instruments mark the rising in power and competence of the practitioner, for each represents the outer symbol of his or her inner achievement. The four instruments, which date back to at least the Middle Ages, if not longer, are the Platter, pentacle or shield; the Cup, chalice or cauldron; the Candle, sword or blade; and the Wand, staff or spear. Each of these instruments is associated with an element of which it is a symbol, although some traditions of Western ritual magic attribute these in different ways. All ways are correct, and as you study and begin to collect your own sets of symbolic instruments, you will become aware of how they are best associated in your own mind.

Often valid magical schools will have a series of grades or degrees, following on from an initiation ceremony, in which the candidate promises to do as she is told in the training and becomes a companion with those already admitted. The degrees are marked by the novice gaining knowledge about each Element in turn, showing skill and inner determination to conquer and understand the power of the Element.

Usually the first Element tackled in this way is Earth. Not only is this the name of our home planet, but it is the foundation and stable form on which everything is built. It represents solidity, strength and endurance, and is an essential Element to understand. You can begin by thinking about things it represents in your own life. Is your home, your family, your job a source of stability and a framework for the future? Are you a practical person, for much magical work is done with your hands? How 'down to earth' are you? How do you value material things? Do you value only objects which you can see and feel, or would you also value thoughts, music and the inspiration which comes from inner sources? All these things are important to the twentieth-century magician and no matter how high you might aspire to rise, you will still need to keep your feet firmly on the ground.

The Element to think about next is Water. Our bodies contain a large amount of water and so, like the sea, we are slightly affected by the pull of the Moon's gravity. Each month subtle aspects of our moods change in response to this invisible influence, most often noticed in the pattern and vividness of our dreams. Another skill to start to develop is to note down every morning whatever fragments of dreams you can recall. The more often you do this, the clearer and more useful these dreams will be. Some even will predict the future, if you learn to watch them. More on this later.

Water is the Element associated with the emotions. As I said before, you have to feel for your magic, or it is a waste of time. Performing a ritual, say to bless a new baby or to consecrate your wedding ring, will often bring tears to your eyes, even if you are a 15-stone rugby-playing man! Magic draws upon an emotional response for some of its power; it can affect the way you feel. I am sure you will remember times when you have been moved by music or some event you have witnessed, whether to tears of joy or feelings of rage and resentment. You may have to learn to cope with these feelings and deal with the tears, but they are a sure sign that you are gaining magical expertise, not that you are being weakened and made soft.

Next usually comes the Element Fire, shown in magical rituals by some sort of living flame, as a candle or lamp. In some circumstances this could be represented by burning incense or joss sticks, but always there is real heat or flame. In us Fire is energy and impulse, it is the active side of our work, as opposed to the quieter meditations. Fire can energize us, giving us strength to overcome our own failings and go on when we are weary. It is the heat within us, the passion which we may have for our beloved and the passion we need to empower our rites, for unless we feel strongly about the causes we are supporting, we are wasting our time. Some of the magical arts do require endurance and vitality and at the end of a hard piece of work we may feel tired, but we will also feel a source of energy which powers the whole universe is available to us, to plug in, as it were, and recharge the batteries. That endless source of unseen energy runs the entire cosmos, and can be manipulated through some magical arts to empower our work once we know how to pay homage to the Light.

The last of the Four Earthly Elements is Air. This is the breath of life which awakens all living things, and it is associated magically with thought, inspiration, which means both to breathe in air and to become aware of new knowledge. Breathing is an important part, as you will have seen, of many exercises of mental magic. By breathing slowly we can become calm, but you need to breathe faster during exertion. Inspiration is also important, for it can give us poetry, insight and the power of intuition, which is the greatest teacher of all. Just by being still and watching our breathing we can become open to sudden bursts of immediate knowledge. This may be in the form of a song, a ritual or some verses for our beloved. It is a situation in which problems can be solved and intuitive guesses made accurately. The mind is not completely understood and it may be that thoughts and many of the seemingly mental processes are not in fact limited to the physical organ which is our brain.

There is a fifth Element which is important to consider, and that is Spirit, or aether, as it is sometimes called in older books. This is the power which is symbolized by the light of a candle on the altar of a ritual. It is the source of power and the link to the deities who are important to every magician. As each of the previous Elements have become less tangible, less dense, so Spirit is invisible, yet it is essential that there is a spiritual quality to the work of magic. As you become more aware, you will discover that you can see or sense in another way the Spirit aspect of your magical circle. It might seem like a tingling sensation or an awareness of light, or even the physical presence of another living being, although you may be alone. The fifth Element is a Mystery, it has to be experienced before you may accept its reality. In magic, as already mentioned, it is not expected that students *believe* anything, rather that, as they gain experience, they widen their own understanding.

You will probably realize that the Four basic Elements are quite closely associated with your body. You could say that the Earth is your physical body, the Water the flow of your blood, the Fire the heat and energy and passion of your heart, and the Air the very breath of life within you. All of this is motivated by the Spirit, the divine spark which is in all humans and is the essence of all gods and goddesses within.

In nature the Four Elements are in balance and the fourfold aspects of our human nature also need to be held in balance, or, if there is something wrong with us, brought into balance.

For example, you may be a very physical person, liking to exert yourself through sport or athletic activities, and find it very hard just to sit down. To bring harmony and peace to your life you will need to use a moving form of meditation rather than the static sitting posture of the Western Tradition. In the olden days many people were able to meditate whilst they performed repetitive tasks out of doors, and the same skill can be used by making a walk a meditation, focusing the mind on a single theme whilst striding along.

If you are very emotional and find your feelings get in the way of clear thinking, again you might find a practical exercise helpful. To bring you down to earth, think of the garden. Gardening, or strolling in parks or other people's gardens, can be calming without affecting emotion. Making pots or clay models can also help, for it involves imagination and practical handicraft. It is important for magicians to be aware of their feelings and not repress them. I know one man who has studied and practised ritual for many years, yet he cannot allow his feelings to enter into his work. He performs elaborate but mechanical rituals which are like the music a musical box plays, tuneful but with no heart. It is feelings, under your own control, which are most effective in ceremonies.

Those people who are very intellectual often have great difficulties with magical work because they have to analyse and reason out everything. Some rituals have to be done in a spirit of experimentation and openness to allow unexpected and spontaneous things to happen. Intellectual people also find it hard to give any credence to the imagination. 'Imagination' comes from the same root as 'magic' and seems to be an aspect of the verb 'to make'. If you want to make something, be it a cake or a suspension bridge, you usually imagine what the outcome should be like – how the cake might be decorated, or the form and structure of the bridge. First you make an image, on paper or in your head, and then from that the design proceeds. To make magic you have to imagine the outcome, the healed person, the new job or the happy relationship. Only by regular practice at awakening this awareness to other possibilities will it be possible to gain any skill in magic.

Very down-to-earth people also suffer from a lack of imagination, not because they do not believe in it, but simply because they never see a use for it. If you are used to making things with ordinary, physical things, it might be hard to start imagining non-solid objects. By waking to your dreams you might become aware of places that do not exist, colours beyond the spectrum and all the regions of the mid-sphere or non-reality where magic is part of existence. Being practical does have advantages – you are far less likely to be carried away by the claims of pseudo-magical teachers who offer instant power, cash or enlightenment, for example, and will be able to make any furniture or adapt candlesticks for use without any difficulty, but you might find it harder to awaken inner vision to divine or to heal, except by hands-on methods, like massage or Touch for Health.

Every sort of character can be an asset to a magical group, for the advantages and difficulties that individuals have are balanced out, but if you are working on your own, as many people tend to be, at least to begin with, you will have to work on yourself to strive for harmony. The exercises at the end of this chapter deal with the Four Elements, and though it may be early in your training, you might like to start to collect symbols of them. This trains your awareness to find a bargain, to use your own intuition and creative abilities.

To begin with, see if you can imagine a place in a shop or market where you might find a candlestick and a cup. Shut your eyes and allow the idea of the object to come into focus, then start to expand so that you begin to see the setting in a way that you can recognize. You can try this exercise last thing at night so that your dreams may be able to show you a source of the things you need. Do recognize that though there are stores which sell magical equipment, tools and necessities, to find these for yourself in other places is a far more rewarding and important experience for you, the trainee magician.

As already mentioned, get used to looking at your dreams as you awaken. Try to wake up naturally rather than being shaken out of your dream world by an alarm. Natural sleep goes in cycles of about 90 minutes, so try to plan your waking up time to allow at least four and a half, six, or seven and a half hours of sleep. In this way you wake in an upcurve of waking and the dreams of the last section will remain clear. To get the best results, if you have to be about at a certain time, go to bed a bit earlier. Relax and realign your thinking by reading for a while before you sleep so that you are able to detach yourself from everyday cares completely. This aids deep and refreshing sleep with clear and complete dreams.

Keep a notebook by your bed with a pen specially for dream notes. At first your jottings may be vague and incomplete, but as you learn the art of conscious dream recall, it will get easier. Use the following exercise to help you.

Exercise Seven

Keeping a Dream Book

This is simply the idea of buying a special Dream Book and a pen which must not stray from beside your bed. Choose a nice book, keep it only for your dreams and re-read it from time to time, for it will record your progress. Even if you only have the dimmest memory of any material, make a note, perhaps, 'I know I dreamt but only remember the colour red or the shape of a triangle...' In time these fragments of form, colour and even feelings will become more vivid and start to make sense.

If you use a diary with dates, this will help you set your nighttime activities against what is happening during the day, or against the Moon phase. The effort of this will train you in the art of magical diary keeping which will be important when you start to add magical ritual to your study. After a month or so, look back and see what you wrote down. You may find that already there is a new clarity, or that some dreams seem to be predictive, as they often are, but go unnoticed because we forget to write down the date.

You may also notice that as the phases of the Moon change each month, so the content and patterns of your dreams follow. Some people have clear and distinct dreams at the full Moon, others about the time of the dark of the Moon or the new Moon. Find out whether these Moon phases affect your dreams, or even the patterns of your emotional and physical energy. Soon you will see improvements.

Exercise Eight

Aligning with the Elements

This is a simple mental exercise to start to align you with the Five Elements. It can be done in the morning and evening, before meditation, or in order to direct your thinking towards a particular idea.

Stand up straight in a room where you won't be disturbed for about 20 minutes. Place your feet firmly on the ground about a shoulder width apart. If you can remain standing with your eyes closed that is best, but some people lose their balance if they try this. If you have to keep your eyes open, look at a neutral surface and let your gaze relax. Start to think about the Earth beneath your feet and consider that, like a tree, your legs and feet connect you with the Earth. See this as the foundation of your body, the strength and endurance which support you. Imagine rocks and great trees as symbols of continuation and time.

Next think about water, fluidity and the cup shape made by the bones of your hips. Your belly processes the fluids you take in, but you may have 'gut feelings' about situations, for it is a seat of emotion. Think about the Holy Grail, that ancient symbol of a cup which brings healing and controls the flow of waters of the Earth, bringing rain after drought. Let your feelings of calmness and a wider awareness flow out.

Then think about the fire of passion, the energy to live and move which comes from your heart. Think about love and what and whom you love, and sense the powerful beating of your heart, driving the energizing red blood around your body, giving you the force of life. See your heart like a moving flame, expanding and contracting and sending out love and life all around you.

Think next about your throat and the power of speech, driven by the air you breathe. Think about inspiration as you breathe in and aspiration, the heights to which you can rise, as you breathe out. Be aware how powerful words can be, whether written or spoken. Recall when words affected you, perhaps as poetry or shouted orders.

Become aware of your thinking processes and the way invisible thoughts flow through the world. See if it is pictures, words or mere concepts which come when you start to think about a problem. Remember some happy event from the past and feel where your eyes move to. Can you visualize the scene or feel the emotion?

Now reach up above your head, mentally, and become aware of the Spiritual Light blazing above you, depicted as a halo in holy images. It is the top part of the aura of light which surrounds everyone and is the link with your higher or inner self, your conscience, the 'still, small voice' within. Feel that light shining down over you like warm sunlight on a still day. Begin to feel energized and balanced by the imagery or feelings which sweep over you.

After a few moments, allow the imagery and the sensations of the Five Elements to slowly flow away, into the ground, so that you feel completely awake and revitalized.

Try this night and morning for several weeks and see if it helps with any health or concentration problems.

Exercise Nine

Earth and Water, Fire and Air

This is a basic meditation exercise which you will need to repeat all through your magical training. Once again it looks at those building blocks of ritual and much practical modern magic, the Elements.

Sit down in your Pharaoh position, take six slow, deep breaths and centre your awareness within you. Close your eyes, relax and allow some image to do with the Earth float into your mind. Think about the soil in which everything grows, think about the creation of the world, think about the changing seasons, but always come back to the single word 'earth'. Try this for four or five days and, like your dream diary, jot down concepts in a meditation book, even if they are vague and fragmented.

For the next five days work on 'water'. What it is, what it does and how you feel about it. Again, write down these thoughts at the end of each session. Think how water moves, how it cycles through seas, rain, earth, rivers, people and eventually back to the seas again.

Later, see what images and concepts are produced when you focus on the word 'fire'. See how different those images and experiences are from 'earth' and 'water'. Think of natural fires, home fires, fire in making and in destruction. Explore it thoroughly for five sessions, always entering some notes at the end of each attempt.

Look next at 'air', the invisible source of life and breath. Feel inspired as you sit relaxed, and still, and quiet, with the air moving around you, in and out of your lungs, and feel the wind of change blowing through your mind.

Finish off this series by using the same form of posture, relaxation and focus to look at the word 'Spirit'. 'The Spirit that moveth on the face of the water...' The spirit which moves you, the spirit of place, or the unseen spirits, fairies, gods and angels which may enter your inner world of vision. Again, note down in words or pictures what you hear, feel, see or experience.

Keep this up as regularly as you can, every day for about a month, and remember to jot down something at the end of every session. At the end of the series, look back at what you have written, maybe adding other ideas that have come to you in a different coloured ink so you can see what was your first impression as against new thoughts or ideas. Finally, think what part of you or your life resonated most closely with each Element and note any changes you have noticed so far.

Chapter Four
The Power of the Planets

'It is hard to believe the personification of the planets
and choice of names could be pure chance...these archetypal forces show mankind's more psychic faculties, and
it is not difficult to realise why these experiences became
projected into the conscious mind as gods, planetary
gods...'

Jeff Mayo, *Teach Yourself Astrology*

Magic works through various systems of symbols, and already I
have mentioned the Four Elements, Earth, Water, Fire and Air.
These relate to our own earthly being, but magic needs to go
beyond the limitations of each individual. For this reason it is
necessary to look at the importance of the seven ancient
planets which form a framework to much practical magic.
Although we are aware that our own solar system, that is, the
number and forms of all the planets which orbit our own star,
the Sun, actually exceeds seven, the 'new' planets are seen,
from a magical point of view, as reflections or expansions of the
older seven. Also several of the 'planets' used in magic are not
actually planets, for this mystical seven includes the Sun, which
is a star, and the Moon, which is our own satellite.

You will know that there are seven days of the week; the
names of those days are taken from the names of the seven
planets in various classical tongues: Monday, the day of the

Moon; Tuesday, the day of Mars, called Tiw in Old Norse; Wednesday, the day of Mercury, called Woden or Odin, again in old Norse; Thursday, the day of Jupiter, Thor of the Norsemen; Friday, the day of Venus, or Frigga, from the Norse; Saturday, the day of Saturn; and finally, Sunday, the day of the Sun. The names of the days of the week are derived from those of gods and goddesses whose powers were thought to be increased or beneficial on their named day. Even now those magicians who make talismans with the powers of the planets built in try to work on the planetary day and in the house when that planet is particularly strong. It is also useful to be able to read an ephemeris, the tables of planetary positions used by astrologers, so that you can calculate the most potent interaction for your magical work. When you are just starting out on your path, however, it is sufficient to recognize that these seven heavenly bodies and the powers they represent and magically pour forth have always been important, and that they are still used today.

The planets are so named because they travel across the heavens in a way that the individual stars do not. In the sky there is a band of stars which contain the constellations which we know as the Signs of the Zodiac which move majestically round our night sky throughout the year. Against this background certain smaller points of light were observed to move, usually forwards but occasionally backwards, against the starry patterns of the night. Like stars, they shine with varying amounts of brightness and Venus, like the Moon, has phases which can be seen with a telescope as she journeys around the Sun.

All the ancient and classical religious systems named these wanderers after their most important deities, judging that the planets could somehow influence people, could respond to prayers or invocations, could empower talismans and bring luck. To each god or goddess they attributed a series of symbols, colours, shapes, numbers and incenses. All these sets of symbols are called 'correspondences' and it is by drawing on knowledge of the appropriate ones that magical work using planetary powers is performed. As you carry on your studies you will probably read the tales of the classical deities of Greece or Rome and begin to see how their stories connect with the correspondences attributed to them. Often illustrated children's books of these heroic tales will give you a clear grasp of their assorted activities and areas of power.

One of the oldest and probably simplest ways of working planetary magic is by the use of coloured candles. Several books have been written on candle magic and if you read them you may be disappointed to find that different authors attribute different colours or numbers to each planet. This is because these attributes are very old and have been derived from various sources, which, having grown up separately, vary from place to place. The authors who write about such matters usually follow one particular tradition which may be different from that learned by another magician. What matters to any practitioner is to be consistent. If you follow the system which attributes the colour green to Venus, for instance, then you will use the colour orange for Mercury, although another system suggests turquoise for Venus and pale blue for Mercury. To confuse things further, there are lots of ways in which numbers are attributed to the planets, based on the Qabalist's Tree of Life or Napoleon's *Book of Fate* or all sorts of ancient systems. The numbers we use come from Arabia and it was the ancient Arab peoples, living under clear, desert skies, who gave the names to many of the stars and tracked their courses.

To begin with, it is enough to look at the days of the week and their natural connections with the planet of their name. This will start to give you a structure upon which you can add new details as you discover them. Gradually it will become necessary to draw up charts of the seven planets and all the things associated with them, because you will need that information at your fingertips to make talismans, to chant spells and to work planetary rituals. Although such ideas may seem old-fashioned and difficult to grasp in an age of computers and modern technology, the old methods work efficiently. Modern magic still uses communication in various ways with these ancient gods and goddesses, and although the diagrams of a talisman may be drawn on a computer screen or the ritual typed on a word processor, what matters is the human-to-god link through your inner mind. That is what makes the spells work, not the technological hardware!

MONDAY

Starting from Monday, what do you associate with the Moon? It shines by night, but also in the day, when the pale crescent may be seen after sunrise or late in the day when the sky is clear. The Moon is always changing, because due to the relationship between the Earth, the Sun and the Moon, a shadow falls across the Moon's face. Like the planets, she shines by reflected sunlight. It is the angle between the Moon and the Sun which gives us the phases. When the Moon circles the Earth she turns the same face to us all the time and at the full Moon, on a clear night, it is possible to see the craters on her pale surface.

The gravity of the Moon as she circles the Earth affects the tides, drawing them towards her, and in a lesser way, because our bodies contain a lot of water, we too are affected. The dark phases of the Moon may make us more psychic or sensitive to things around us, for the Moon has traditionally influenced matters of the inner mind. Lunacy is named after the idea that many mentally disturbed people are more manic at full Moon, and that those so disturbed have changes in mood and behaviour as the lunar month passes. The Moon also affects bleeding, and some enlightened surgeons, who have become aware of this, schedule more extensive operations at times when the Moon is less likely to cause a bleeding problem.

Many women's menstrual cycles also link in with the Moon, although few women have an exact match to the 29 and a bit days of the lunation as seen on Earth. It has been found that communities of women living close together adjust their cycles so that they bleed at the same time. In times past, women at this time were thought of as harbingers of the Devil and capable of turning milk sour by just looking at it. In some societies they were shut away and had to be ritually cleansed at the end of their period before returning to their homes. Nowadays, many women who have studied magic and the psychic arts have discovered that they may be empowered at different times in their menstrual cycle, having vivid dreams and clear visions, for example, at a certain time. Since the start of this century more and more women have risen to high places in magical circles, and have drawn their own feminine powers into making them wise and strong. Dion Fortune, who founded one of the most important magical schools, The Society of the Inner Light, was trained by some of the women in the earlier Hermetic Order of the Golden Dawn. She wrote a novel called *Moon Magic* and was well aware of the magical significance of our satellite, working with it to bring inspiration and retrieve ancient sources of angelic wisdom.

The magical powers of the Moon are concerned with all the psychic skills, which include scrying or crystal gazing, divination with the Tarot cards or with similar picture systems, and some forms of healing. Using the Moon's light, it is possible to bless water or other liquids used in ritual, by reflecting moonlight into it with a mirror. Also mirror magic, used for protection and for far seeing, can be helped by lunar energies. The Moon can help people to become more sensitive in a psychic way, so that it is easier to psychometrize objects, to read their history just by holding them. A similar gain may be had when reading the lines on the palm of someone, because you are touching them as well as making a divination from the lines, shapes and markings on the fingers and hands.

The different phases of the Moon are powerful adjuncts to practical magic, because, like the tides in the sea, which the Moon impels, there is a natural ebb and flow of energies. When the Moon is waxing, growing in the sky, it is a time to encourage things which need to expand. It used to be common to plant flower seeds and those for vegetables and fruit which thrived above ground during the waxing phase of the Moon. When she waned, it was right to plant potatoes, carrots, root vegetables and any other plants which needed to establish deep roots for success. The light of the Moon was also needed for healing: as she grew, the health and strength of the patient would be encouraged, and as she waned to the dark of the Moon, disease, heat and swellings would be prompted to follow suit and shrink away.

Magical work performed on a Monday often includes meditations which seek knowledge from your deep, inner mind, meditations which help you awaken your latent psychic talents and encourage hunches to be noticed. These meditations are often very vague and intangible, like moonlight upon still water, yet they can eventually become very rewarding and enlightening.

On Mondays, because it is the start of the working week, it is useful to follow the Moon tides, waxing and waning. With the growing Moon, work on projects or tasks which have an outward effect, which have to be shared with other people, and in the waning fortnight, get on with filing, the sorts of jobs you need to work on alone and anything more personal than public. By becoming aware of these tides in your dreams, you will find they are easy to work with the rest of the time.

TUESDAY

The next day, Tuesday, comes under the rulership of the planet Mars. Mars is responsible for wars, disputes, energy, transport, iron (his metal) and anything concerned with industry. Because conflict of one sort or another is still common in everyday life, from the trivial spats we have with our family over TV programmes to the all-out hatred and anguish raised by divorce, Mars can be a potent force in the modern world.

Because the whole of Nature is a dynamic but balanced system, it is necessary to learn that there is a need for what may seem to be disturbing forces alongside the more obviously beneficial powers in our universe. There has to be energy, loyalty, pride and the power to defend as well as the active energies used to destroy, burn and break down barriers. If there were no powers of destruction, our world could be lived on an increasing pile of undecayed dinosaurs, trees and every other thing which has ever lived on Earth! But the destruction of one thing can be the production of something else. By burning coal we produce heat and energy. By decaying, leaves and animal remains produce useful and nourishing chemicals for the growth of new plants and the fruits they provide. Some things need force to break them down, others need time, that other great power of the planets, Saturn, which is seen, with Mars, by some as difficult. It is necessary to know that even the breaking of silence in a conversation which can lead to friendship is just as much under the dominion of Mars as is the broken treaty which leads to war. Friendship and amity are the opposite sides of the same coin. Mars, the red planet and the God of War, can bring peace by ending deadlock, bring new advances by breaking old taboos and energize the forces of spring to overwhelm with green the dark forces of winter.

Mars will bring energy and fire to magical work, and will help with many practical matters, from job prospects to health. Anywhere you need energy and drive to get something going you can call upon Mars. He will help with settling quarrels and with kick-starting projects, especially anything mechanical, made of steel, or fiery in its nature. Often to succeed at something requires just the effort of getting started and overcoming the inevitable inertia which stalls many of life's larger projects. To write a book requires a good kick of Mars energy, because it is a long-term project, using mechanical equipment, and one which can lead to all sorts of mental debates in its completion.

If you are involved in a legal situation where the various parties have taken opposing sides, the power of Mars can unblock the log-jam, because as well as war, Mars rules over justice. All situations will have a just outcome, maybe not always in your favour, but justice is an eternal verity, like love or war. Mars can give you strength and the power to endure unfavourable developments in life, but because he wields a mighty and destructive force, you need to learn how safely to call upon the assistance he can give. One way we all exhibit our own Martian qualities is through anger and losing our tempers. To call upon Mars we must have our own strong feelings under control or the essential drive his symbols can offer will overwhelm us and leave us unable to cope. In every sort of magic it is important to be aware of the possible outcome of any spell, so meditating on the roaring, red power of Mars before you ask him for help will show you that wild fury may not advance your cause, whereas cool, predetermined action will succeed.

WEDNESDAY

Wednesday is the province of the subtle and elusive Mercury, who, like the liquid metal named after him, can trickle away just when you thought you had control. Mercury is the great communicator, the far-ranging traveller, the messenger of the gods, but he also rules over thieves and con-men. The ancient Greeks called him Hermes and the Egyptians in the time of the Pharaohs named him Thoth. He gave his name to Hermetics, a wide-ranging branch of magic using ceremony and inner communication with hidden powers. Mercury, in Britain, is also the name of a telecommunications system!

Quite a lot of magical work requires communication of one sort or another. Often it is the basic meditative communication between our own inner or subconscious mind and our waking awareness, or it could be communication with unseen teachers, gods and goddesses, angels or elemental beings. Sometimes it is reactivating a communion with the past or with other people at a distance. It could be the various arts of divination, which make a bridge of words and images with the Tarot card illustrations, the divinity of the tradition, and our own perceptions, or by random pictures in a crystal ball or scrying mirror. Mercury can reveal to us wisdom in the pages of a book, arcane answers in a TV programme or intuition through the everyday media, if we make a direct request for his help.

Mercury moves fast, too, and the swiftest international communications come under his jurisdiction. Technically Mercury is not a 'he', for this power is hermaphrodite. Once again this is a symbol of transformation, from male to female, from person to person, from continent to continent and from mind to mind, even if one of these is human and the other a god. Through change, that absolutely essential aspect of all magic, Mercury brings about what we wish to alter. Through communication he brings enlightenment and the wisdom of hermetic magic.

Unlike some of the other planetary powers, Mercury is hard to pin down. His activities cover a wider span of human and divine arts, but his shape is ephemeral, his movements invisible and his effects mainly on the subtle levels of the mind. Consciousness, in its broadest sense is within the remit of this wing-heeled god. Many of the thinking processes, which too involve the microscopic chemical and electrical connections in our brains, come under his spell, and certain dreams, especially of travel, may be messages he is trying to send to our waking minds. A lot of actual magical work goes on during times of altered states of consciousness, from the calm relaxation of personal meditation to the shared patterns of ritual when the mind perceives a different setting from that which the body inhabits. It could well be that it is Mercury, in one of his many forms, whom you call upon to gain mastery of these subtle levels of your own awareness.

In the outer world Mercury can be invoked to aid on journeys in the way that Catholics call upon their Saint Christopher to protect them. He can help keep your car on the road or the train to its timetable. He can find ways of directing you to a safe parking space, and, thief that he may be, he might be asked to invisibly stand guard over your vehicle or belongings. I tell you, much stranger things have been asked by modern magicians! Mercury can help with communications, finding phone numbers in the book or even setting up 'coincidental' meetings between old friends who have lost touch. Call upon Hermes if you just can't find that address and 'Presto!' a phone call or letter puts you in touch again. Want some unusual piece of information? Well, again Hermes is your deity. Send out a mental cry on a Wednesday and who knows, within a few hours you can have your answer, even if it seems very unlikely. The communication business is not only limited to earthly pursuits.

THURSDAY

Thursday is ruled over by Jupiter, Zeus-Pater, the all father, sky god and great businessman of the cosmos. Jupiter may be symbolized by an oak tree and the lightning that strikes it, but he is the expert on growth, both in the natural world and in the field of finance. If it is an increase in cash or position or power that you want, then it should be to Jupiter that you address your invocations. To gain his favour will require work, that four-letter word most of us try to avoid, but four is his number (at least in some of the most useful systems of numerology!)

Jupiter is the largest planet in our solar system and so is the symbol of expansion and plenty. As father of the gods he is a kindly deity whose actions are always for the benefit of those who ask for help. Thursday is the best day of the week to try to stabilize financial matters, to ask for a rise in pay or to set about launching a new business venture. Because Jupiter's number is four, it represents the square shape, also a sign of stability and strength which is needed as the foundation to any expansive enterprise. The gains brought by the influence of this mighty planet tend to be slow growth rather than explosive change, so the work that you need to put in to make a success of a project will have to carry on for a while, and it is best to realize this before you request help from Jupiter. If you have an immediate problem, he may move too slowly to get you out of the mess, but if you plan ahead and need longer-term advances, then this would work for you.

FRIDAY

Friday is ruled by the beautiful planet Venus, whose rising in the morning or evening, because she is close to the Sun, also gives her the name Star of the Morning, or Evening Star, depending where she is in her cycle. Venus, as Goddess of Love, naturally rules over affairs of the heart, but she also looks after other sorts of partnerships, like friendship, business companions and people who share team activities. Anything to do with increased harmony, peace (which is victory after conflict) and general contentment can be achieved by asking favours from her.

Many people think that magic can help with their love affairs, and appeal to Venus or carry out rituals in Fridays using her colours and symbols, but they often do not look beyond their own immediate desires. Partnership, under the rulership of Venus, has to be equal and to impel other people to love you or to change their lives to suit your whims is at best grey and at worst black magic. Free will is vital to the effectiveness of spells and to try to coerce others into doing your bidding is not allowing free will. If you happen to fall for someone but she does not return your advances, you need to consult the wisdom of Venus, perhaps by mirror magic or by reading the cards, to get advice on how best to behave. If you are willing to change yourself, as the guidance you receive teaches you, then you can become more desirable, more worthy of love and the affection you crave. If the first person you have set your heart on is not available or really is not the one for you, then Venus can guide you, with the early morning light or by her shining at twilight, towards a more suitable and enduring partner.

Beauty is both in the eye of the beholder and within you. Venus can help in both cases, for her power can allow you true sight to see the person you fancy as they really are, and from that decide whether they are as you wish or whether a glamour has covered your eyes. To ask Venus for help can give you a lot of self-confidence, and that will certainly lead to you being able to find friends and lovers with whom you can have a lasting relationship. The mirror of Venus can show you what you are really like, and, if you have courage, you can see how to change your outlook or image to gain confidence and determination.

Venus is also concerned with relationships within a family, so that she can help you understand your children and the new ideas they may be bringing into your home. She can bring insights into difficult situations, help you control your temper, and lead you to more peaceful and harmonious situations, if you give her a chance. Partnerships in all aspects of life can be aided by Venusian power and this also applies to magical groups, which are very like families. There has to be a closeness and trust among your lodge brothers and sisters because that harmony will power the rituals. If you do not trust your companions or can't feel at ease in their company, then the work you do will have less power. In really well established magical lodges, or the covens of witches, there is a mutual love and trust and deep friendship which has few equivalents in everyday life. You may feel set apart through an interest in the occult, but this can also lead to a sense of belonging, and of coming home, when you meet up with the right people.

Many novels about magical subjects seem to suggest that there is a lot of sex and sexual aspects of ritual in magic, but that is actually just fiction. There is love, there is openness, there is a whole range of deep feelings, but these are not sexual. In groups there may be a number of married pairs, but their intimate relationships are not exploited in magical work. Certainly there are writers who go on about sex magic, but most of them don't know anything about the true magical relationships which go far beyond a physical union. (The arts and rituals of Tantra, an Indian form of worship and practice, usually dedicated to Kali, the Goddess of Love and War, do not come within the Western Mystery Tradition and so are not dealt with here. To become a Tantric master requires a very long apprenticeship to forms of yoga and self-control which few people from the West ever gain.)

SATURDAY

The next day, Saturday, comes under the rulership of Saturn, the original Time Lord and keeper of records. Saturn is responsible for everything to do with ageing, with boundaries, with structures and things which are expected to endure. Many people think that the influences of this large, dark planet are the hardest to put up with, yet Saturn is a great helper. In any activity where it is necessary to keep on going, or when you are having to deal with older people, or when you need to set limits for yourself, the aid that you can gain is immense.

There are many activities in magic when it is necessary to consult the Akashic Records, the hidden knowledge and experiences of the entire human race throughout its long history on Earth. We each have our own personal memories and recollections, but the Akashic Records contain everything. Each individual has a right to consult these data banks on her own behalf. You may have read about 'past life recall' when an individual is helped to remember who she has been in previous lives or to seek out, through 'far memory', the roots of today's fears or phobias. There are systems of therapy based on this kind of regressive memory. However, if an individual seeks to recall previous lives in which she has been involved in magic, or to trace skills in healing, or other useful but forgotten talents, then there are rites to Saturn which can be used.

Saturn is also responsible for debts and one of the Saturnian angels, Cassiel, can be asked to help sort out long-term financial situations.

All kinds of ordinary responsibilities come under the influence of Saturn, especially the lengthy ones. Many young people find it hard to work with this dark energy, but as you get older the strengths of stability and the knowledge that you can endure become more important. Old people can also gain from the inherent powers of this planet with its silvery rings, because all the wisdom and practical experiences they have built up during their lives can be put to best use by the actions of Saturn. He is the giver of patience, constancy and long-term support in a way that none of the other planets can match.

SUNDAY

The last day of the week, Sunday, is, of course, ruled by the Sun, the star around which all our solar system revolves. The Sun, along with the Moon, is the most obvious influence upon our world. It shines to give us daylight, the seasons are ruled by the Sun, and the growth of plants, and so the whole food chain, is dependent on solar light. For these reasons the Sun is magically responsible for all the outgoing things in our life, our confidence, our position as the star in our own heavenly circle of family and friends, and much more. The Sun is the symbol of life and so is used a great deal in healing rituals.

We all like to bask in the sunlight or take holidays where the skies are blue and there is warmth and light and bright colours, because in most cases, these things make us feel well. In the dark, dim days of winter we feel shut in and miserable, and long for heat and light. The Sun rules the pattern of our waking state and though these days we don't usually toil in the fields from sunrise to sunset, our usual activities take place in daylight.

The Sun is a male deity in most places and in most magical systems, although in northern traditions the Sun is female, and, as in the nursery rhyme, there is a Man in the Moon. In Japan there is a Sun Goddess and a Moon God, and in some of the early Egyptian pantheons of deities the Lord of the Moon is male. The character of the Sun, however, is to do with self-esteem and self-awareness and applies equally to male and female magicians. Solar ideas are all about the first person, the self and personal direction.

The Sun has been used as a powerful religious symbol for many regions in the world. The ancient Egyptians reverenced Ra, the Sun God, and saw that he had several forms at different times of the day: Ra-Harahkte, the God of the Rising Sun, Horus, the hawkheaded God of the Day, Tum at sunset, and, during the night, Kephra, the sacred scarab beetle who carried the Sun through the Underworld to re-emerge at dawn.

The Druids in the western part of Europe in pre-Christian times called upon the Sun in the sky as a symbol of the Great God of Light, and held their rituals 'in the light of day and in the face of the Sun'.

The Romans called the Sun God Apollo, who, legend tells, brought the power of music and of healing to the Earth. The Greeks worshipped Helios, who drove his four-horse chariot through the daytime sky, spreading beneficence and plenty over all the land. Early Christian texts also speak of Jesus as 'the Light of the World', and in many other old sacred writings the idea of light and enlightenment were signs of spiritual gifts. In many religious pantheons there were sets of father and mother and child gods and goddesses, and worshippers were urged to feel that they were also children of the gods they prayed to and in whose honour ceremonies were held.

Healing is often done using the Sun, if there is sunlight which the sick person can experience or symbols which represent the Sun, such as a lighted gold or yellow candle, a golden mirror to reflect the light or a talisman made of the metal gold, or gold-coloured materials. In many cases not only can the body be healed by this Sun power, but it can work on the moods and feelings, especially after disappointments or instances of failure. By boosting a person's morale and self-esteem, she can be helped to her feet.

As you become more knowledgeable about the powers of the various planets you will see how you can ask them for help. You do not need to believe that these moving lights in the sky are actually living deities, but to come to recognize them as forces, channels of focused power, or symbolic objects from which certain kinds of energy or guidance can flow. Ancient people felt that strange forms of energy, information or power beamed out with the light from many heavenly bodies. They built vast stone structures, like the monolithic monuments of Stonehenge and

Avebury in England, New Grange in Ireland and the vast temples as far away as Malta, North Africa and Crete. Most of these huge structures have alignments which point to particular stars, including the rising or setting of our own Sun. The pyramids of Egypt may be set out in the patterns of stars, and tiny tunnels built right through the structure seem to align with stars in the constellation, Orion, seen as their great god, Osiris, or to Sirius, the Dog Star, symbol of Isis, his wife and sister. Power from those stars was gathered and the spirits of the dead Pharaohs were sent back to them, so far memory tells us. Science may not yet have unravelled all these strange concepts, but magical thinking allows that power may be received from planets and from stars, and that they are a source of wisdom and guidance.

No one makes planetary talismans today without knowing that there is some unseen way in which they will help to bring about what is desired. It is an ancient form of magic and those occultists who use the formulas handed down for hundreds of years would assert that talismans can be effective. The effort involved in any form of magic means it is not used unless it is likely to be effective. Although our arts and crafts are ancient they still work and, properly used, like any other practical skill, deliver results as expected.

Exercise Ten

Weekday Magic

Using the information given in this chapter, try to decide what sorts of magic you might do each day of the week. Can you think of a way of working on a single project each day for a week, using the power of each planet in turn to add power to your spell? Which day would you begin?

Exercise Eleven

Gods and Goddesses for Today

Once again get into your meditative position and frame of mind. Close your eyes and think about each planetary power in turn. How would you see, in modern terms, the Goddess of the Moon? Perhaps as a fashion model, always changing her clothes and appearance, or as a wise crone offering predictions seen in a moon-lit crystal ball? What would the Sun God look like and how would the hermaphrodite Mercury appear to you?

Work through all the forms of these ancient deities, and then, one at a time, imagine you are having a conversation with them in a place suitable to each. Mars might be a soldier on a battle-field, Venus a beauty in a paradisical setting, Saturn an old man in a dark cave full of the jewels of hoarded wisdom. How would you talk to them, what might you ask them to help you with? How real do they appear to you?

This is a valuable exercise, so try it sincerely and conscientiously until you get useful answers.

Exercise Twelve

Deities in People

Try to decide which of the deities the people you meet everyday are most like. Do those in authority have the feeling of Jupiter, even if they are women? What about members of your family or your friends, are they behaving like gods and goddesses, and if so, which? Which are you most like or would you like to become one of these ancient deities? (Some of the answers may reflect the influence of the planets in these people's horoscopes.)

Chapter Five
The Way of Ritual

'Although one should not alter a ritual without good reason...it remains that the practising magicians often make use of rituals constructed by themselves. ...if a rite is properly constructed then it can be of the greatest value to those who use it...'

W. E. Butler, *Magic and the Magician*

Ritual is one of the many fragments which make up the work of the practical occultist and witch in today's world. Ritual is an ancient form of specific actions, movements and words which has a particular effect. Often there is no direct link between the pattern of the ritual and the eventual, desired outcome. For example, making a talisman with a circle of gold, engraving someone's name on it, blessing it with frankincense, dedicating it with gesture and chanting to the Sun God doesn't *seem* to cause the healing of that person, yet it does happen.

Every ritual has a specific and predetermined purpose, and all the symbols used in it – the colours, numbers of candles, kinds of gums burned as incense, sort of music played and many other factors – focus in on one single idea, the reason for that ritual. Whether there is only one practitioner or a large group, their aims are in harmony and the entire focus during the ritual is on the predetermined purpose. Of course this harmony has to be gained by people learning the pattern of the ritual and being willing to play the part allotted to them. With small groups (and the majority of working magical groups are fairly small, these days, because they have to fit into modern rooms rather than stately homes), the necessary harmony is easier. Even if you are having to practise on your own you will be able to try out simple and safe basic rituals, so that you learn to feel the changes in atmosphere and the way that spells work out in real life.

Rituals are actually parts of our everyday lives, because we often act in a particular way to bring about a desired result, when the action is not clearly related to the end result. Take turning on a light, for example. Simply pressing a switch turns on the electric bulb, but we don't know how electricity actually works, we don't have to make the wire ourselves, nor do we design the circuits it runs in. A magical ritual works in the same way. We don't have to understand in detail how the spell we speak is circulated around the inner powers, we don't need to define each aspect of what we have asked for and know where it will come from, but we do have to ask clearly, precisely and magically, and the unseen forces will cause what we want to happen. With the light we need to know that if we press the switch the light will come on. If the bulb is dead or if there is a power cut, then our action may go unrewarded. The same is true in magic. We may conduct a perfect ritual, ask clearly for what we desire, yet somehow, because of things we have not anticipated, the spell goes unanswered. We can check the words, the actions and inspect our talisman and so on, but if the unseen force, like the electricity, has not been conducted, then our efforts will be in vain. Magical training is the way to ensure that spells have their desired results.

That is why books and teachers who give brief instructions on how to perform a spell for money or a new car don't work. You do need to understand the pattern of ritual and to know what each part is there for. Just copying some sort of ritual out of a book in isolation, rather than coming to it well informed as the result of much previous study, can prove dangerous. All rituals have an effect upon the people working them, because it is the practitioners' emotions and attitudes which help to direct the power of the ritual. It is also their changed mental focus which makes it possible to see what is happening, watch the flows of power around the sacred circles and observe how the magical energy is leading to success. Because magicians are in a very sensitive frame of mind during this process, they are open to subtle influences from inner powers. When they are trained, they are able to ensure that what they sense is 'good' and helpful; if they have simply worked a ritual from a book, parrot fashion, they may well be open to hidden forces. In that case they will have far less control over what happens and it can feel very frightening. Also, they won't be able to change their ritual to benefit from powers they have invoked, if they can't see them.

Working magic is like driving a racing car. Many people can drive an ordinary car on the road, which is like everyday life, but very few can manage the Formula One vehicles without lots of training and practice. The same is true with occult work. It is not dangerous, but things move a lot faster than in everyday situations and a small lack of concentration can cause trouble. If you really want to become an adept and master all the practical arts of magic, you can, but it does take time and care and patience. By making sure you can enter a meditative state at will and be in contact with aspects of your higher self regularly, you make a clear pathway through your mind, along which safe guidance and wisdom will start to flow.

Ritual has been used in ceremonies of religions and magic for many thousands of years. Even the people who lived in caves and made stone implements seem to have had rituals, particularly around the burial of special dead people. In many parts of the world ancient graves have been found with objects used in daily life, flowers and coloured powders spread on the body. This shows that care was taken and that it mattered to the people still alive. They must have thought that the spirit of the dead person would need a drinking cup, a spear or some simple jewellery in the afterlife. There may have been some sort of feast too, for the carved bones of food animals were often found in the same location.

We don't know what our ancient ancestors were doing or what they believed, but from cave paintings and rock carvings there are images which speak to us across the millennia. Pictures show hunts of food animals, but often the feet of the animals point downwards as if they were already dead, magically ensuring that the hunt would be successful. Other pictures seem to show magicians having trance-like visions, for the figures shown have jagged outlines. Today people who suffer from migraine headaches and those who are trained to go into trance see shapes with these same auroras or black-and-white lightning-like edges. This seems to show that some early magicians were able to lift their spirits out of their bodies and perhaps fly over the landscape to seek out quarry for the hunters. By being able to fly with their minds (and many of the figures are in a horizontal position), maybe they could soar over the countryside, finding fresh water or ripe fruits and seeds, or even make contact with other bands of wandering people in a safe way.

Often very early forms of fat female figures, which anthropologists tend to call 'cult figures' or 'earth goddesses', hold their hands in a particular position. Research by modern magicians has shown that if students get into a meditative frame of mind and then take up one of those postures, it changes the way their visions come. It would seem that each of the postures of these extremely ancient figures has a meaning and will induce in properly prepared people a particular feeling of power, healing or communication with their deities. More work needs to be done on this. Also, using the pictures from the Egyptian temples showing worshippers and priests and priestesses in ritual settings, it is possible to re-enact the same experiences and gain the same sort of healing or awakening power. Even today the position in which you sit during a ritual, the gestures you make and the magical signs which you trace in the air to consecrate your working space all have a particular meaning and need to be done correctly.

Most early ritual was concerned with religion. The actual ceremonies were carried out by trained priestesses and priests who, in Egypt for example, may have worn head-dresses of the various deities in order to enact them for the congregation of ordinary people. By using ritual drama, scenes from the stories of the gods could be shown to the people, who could understand what was happening as the seasons passed or as a special feast was celebrated. The priests or priestesses took on the god form with a mask, which, because it was a magical object, imbued them with the power of that particular deity. It was a ritual act, for example, to assume the head of Anubis, the Guide for Souls, God of the Otherworld, because the priest would then speak and act as if he were Anubis.

This same empowerment by masks forms parts of many religious ceremonies all over the world. Look in any anthropological collection in a museum and you will find carved and decorated masks from every continent. Africa, China and North America, distant Tibet and the Morris dances of Britain, all have their ritual forms to wear on sacred occasions. The Greek theatre in early times also used masks of gods and heroes, for this was a religious rather than an entertaining performance. Most Greek theatres were parts of temples of healing. The actors who put on the character masks, called *Personae*, prayed to them before each play and only when they felt there was a rapport did they don them and commence the drama.

Recently the word 'persona' has been used by psychologists to describe the face we all put on to show the world, our outward-looking mask, while most people have an inner, hidden and secret face, a face of their true selves, which is never shown to the world. The magician acquires yet another mask which shows her true face, the face to show to the gods and angels. At the start of all rituals, as the robes and other regalia are put on, the magician puts on her true self, her perfected and magical self to whom failure is unknown. Sometimes this is called the 'magical personality' or 'true self' and it is in this guise that all magicians operate during ritual. Becoming able to assume this aspect of self takes time and dedication, but without it rituals are mere plays or dramatic games. It is this magical self which acquires a 'magical name', known only in some cases to the individual and the gods.

A true magician has to gain a vision of her magical self and be given, usually by the gods of the tradition she is working, a new name or motto, setting out her aspirations in the Great Work. These are often both the result of a genuine initiation, where those performing the ceremony and the candidate are all prepared by previous work and instruction. Becoming an initiate is the first step in becoming a player in the Great Game of Life. 'Initiation' means to 'enter in', so it is early step, which is often to be repeated throughout life. It is what makes some move from being an 'outsider' to being an 'insider', one empowered with secret knowledge. To undergo formal initiation into a valid magical group or coven is a great honour, and a step not to be taken lightly, without due thought and commitment. There are all sorts of initiating groups in the world today and if it is your own desire to become an initiate, then you will have to take steps to seek out such a path.

Not all initiations which are valid have to be given by other people; some can happen as part of an individual training programme, others can happen as a result of whatever everyday life throws at you. A true and effective initiation occurs when the candidate receives a genuine contact with unseen powers. No amount of drama and sword waving, no amount of money, no amount of high-sounding titles held by the initiator will bring this about if the candidate is not spiritually and mentally ready for it to happen. It is another aspect of the saying 'When the pupil is ready, the teacher will arrive.' In the case of initiation, the teacher is often invisible and a dweller in another realm, but the ceremony or inner experience arrived at by self-initiation puts the candidate and a master into direct contact. Often, at the time, very little is felt to have happened, yet gradually you will find that your whole life has been altered and it is as if you had new glasses through which to view the world or had suddenly discovered a seventh sense. Everything has somehow changed, both within you and in the ordinary world around you. It can be a scary experience, because you find that you have the power to make changes, perhaps to heal, to understand the inner meanings of quite ordinary things. You have a new dimension to your life.

There is no going back, either, because once you have moved into the unseen world of magical reality you can never entirely be shut out. This is a good reason for not rushing in to join the first group or coven you come across. A magical group is often closer than a family and initiation into a coven can be as serious an undertaking as getting married – and can be an even longer-term commitment. Certainly you can leave a lodge or coven if your conscience dictates, no matter what anyone might say to the contrary, but it would be a wrench and would need effort to break the invisible bonds created by having taken such a considered step in the first place. All true magical groups develop what is sometimes called a 'group mind', as do families and partnerships. Each person contributes something to this enclosing spiritual net and each is to some extent affected by it. It produces harmony of purpose and increases the power of the group mind manyfold, but it can particularly influence a newcomer, who usually takes time to acclimatize to it. If there is a period of study and 'getting to know you' before someone is taken in, then the transition from being an 'outsider' to becoming an 'insider' and initiate is gentle, as it should be. Sudden and unprepared initiations can lead to problems, so do be careful if such is offered to you.

Many rituals are relatively simple and can be performed alone or with non-initiated friends. In fact, the largest proportion of magical work by both ceremonial magicians or witches is done in this way, with varying results. A lot of people do read a few books, gather a few of the items they describe and launch themselves, willy-nilly, into a ritual. Often the result of this is failure and some folk then give up the whole idea of magic because, they say, it doesn't work. Would they react in the same way if faced with written instructions on playing a musical instrument, I wonder? Hold the violin in the left hand so that it rests under the chin and your fingers can depress the strings, hold the bow at an angle in the right hand and draw it across the strings, and this will help you play the instrument like Yehudi Menuhin! Really! Yet people treat magical texts in the same way. Sadly, they do not realize that in order for you to get any spell or ritual to work you do need to know the symbols which act as a kind of inner telephone number to attract the attention of the hidden powers, who, in turn, will make it work. Otherwise you are just performing drama without intent.

The safest way to master practical magic in the modern world is to act slowly and carefully. You may need instant results, but until you at least understand the basics, you won't achieve anything worthwhile. To communicate with the angels, ancient gods and powers, you will need to take steps to approach their realms and this is usually achieved by meditation. This may not sound very much fun, but if you learn to become still, silent and open to inner guidance, you will find that you are shown the proper and most effective steps to take towards whatever the aim of your ritual might be. All these things are becoming rarer in our frantic world and so it becomes harder for magic to succeed.

The second most valuable asset to any form of magical work is that of visualization, creative imagery or inner vision. Most young people are able to 'day-dream', that is, whilst in a relaxed frame of mind, enter into an imaginary landscape and perhaps have adventures there. Some people simply allow their mind to drift, when they are bored, and find that colours, shapes and images appear before their inner eyes. This, when under complete control, is one of the most powerful assets to magic and ritual. What happens is that by awakening your imagination, the magic of your creative skills is set loose. The words 'magic', 'image', 'make' and 'imagination' all come from the same root.

Without imagination no one would create anything, from a bridge to a poem to a song or a housing estate. Someone had to have a vision, put it on paper and get it created. Magic is exactly the same. Create in your mind's eye whatever you wish to happen, work your spell and (if not exactly 'Hey, presto!') it will come into being. This sounds very simple. It *is* very simple, but it is not easy!

Magical work involves creating a special place in your inner vision or discovering somewhere which is already there, often referred to as 'a place between the worlds'. This is between the worlds of waking and sleeping, day and night, the everyday world and the worlds within. It may seem like an ancient Egyptian temple with its carved or painted gods, it might be a clearing in the Wildwood, home of the old magics of Europe, it might be an empty, whitewashed room filled with sunlight or a facsimile of the Star Temples of Atlantis. Sometimes these visionary places have to be conjured, literally built mentally, stone by stone, sometimes they just appear to our relaxed and inward-looking vision. If you are being trained in a particular tradition of High or Low magic, there will be an inner landscape which is relevant and helpful which will be shown to you by your teachers. If you are alone, you will have to mentally voyage and, when you see another place, you will have to find out where it is.

In the Western Mystery Tradition one symbolic realm is the vast and trackless forest, seen as the background to the Grail Quest and King Arthur's Camelot. Here you can encounter heroes as knights in armour, goddesses as the guardians of sacred springs and fountains, and wise hermits and talking animals. Here you can find the inspiration of Ceridwen's cauldron with its enchanted potion, for her cauldron is an earlier form of the Christian Grail/Chalice. You can encounter challenges and discover treasures, magical, mundane and spiritual. This wilderness place is what Europe was originally like, wild and sacred, full of animals, birds and power. In visions and inner journeys it is easy to return there to seek out friends on the path, guides or even animal companions.

Other sacred places, which often turn up if you set out to find them in dreams or meditations, are castles, or sometimes the Chapel in the Green, the Hall of the Round Table, or a secret place, entered through a long barrow or ancient burial mound. These places may lead to encounters with Wayland the Smith or Volund or Hephestus or Vulcan, the Maker God in whose forge all things were created. If you find yourself in an orchard of flowering or fruiting trees you could be in Avalon, the Isle of Apples, in which heroes find their rest, or where the Hesperides guard a golden treasure, or even the Garden of Eden, that first paradise, our true human home. Each of these inner places has an exalted position within the Western Mystery Tradition and if it reveals itself to you, you are on the right track.

If you don't get a clear picture or feeling of the magical place, then you will have to choose one and build in your imagination a way to get there. If you choose the Wildwood, find a natural path that leads from your home to a wooded place. If you prefer one of the ancient stone temples, you will need to discover a door to it in any wall near your home. Try this and see what you can find, just by wandering around your own neighbourhood during a quiet period, looking for clues which will lead you, mentally, to the sacred place you seek. Often it takes a while to work on this, but one day, suddenly, a visionary door will open and you will find your way to a place, which is both a surprise and yet familiar. Most of these inner realms are where we go in dreams, so they seem well known when you discover them deliberately.

Once you have found your secret forest or inner temple you will have to hold that vision whilst you call for the kind of help you need. This might be a teacher, a healer, a guide through the labyrinth of magical training or whatever you need. Ask and someone or something will hear. You may well find that a veiled figure approaches. The first thing you must do is to find out who they are, what their name might be. This sounds simple, but requires skill and persistence. You do need to find out who you are dealing with, for many of the inner plane beings are tricksters and will confuse you or lead you a merry dance to no purpose. Try to see what you feel about the figure, whether it seems threatening or friendly (though helpful guides can still look frightening at first glance). See if you can get answers to your questions, which, because this is a visionary experience, will sound like voices or ideas forming in your own head. Test what you learn. Is it helpful? Is it what you need to know? Do you feel you trust the visitor? Be certain you feel safe and comfortable with anyone who gives you advice. This applies equally to real, human teachers or books or any other source of instruction. Ask questions if you want to and expect to get valid answers.

Although seeking inner guidance is an early step in practical magic, as much in today's scientific world as it was in the Middle Ages, there are lots of other simple spells and rituals novices will want to try, whether they have sufficient knowledge or experience to do them safely or not. These often involve changing some annoying factor in life, sorting out a romantic entanglement or making some money. Certainly magic can be a valuable asset in these situations, but it is necessary to look at the moral implications first. Magic does not create anything out of nothing. Every change it is possible to make using occult means still involves real things or people. For example, you cannot make room to park your car in a crowded city by causing another vehicle to fade into thin air! (How would you like it if your car vanished?) You need, in that instance, to be able to magically 'guess' when a space will occur at the time you require. If you ask the Gods of Travel, Mercury or Hermes, for help, or the God of iron mechanical objects, Mars, to find you a place *and listen to their answers*, you will always 'be lucky'. You will get a 'hunch' where to go and nine times out of ten you will be successful.

If you want to sort out someone who is annoying you, think about the situation from her point of view. Does she have reason to upset you? Do you upset her? If you want to actually morally solve this sort of problem, you have to look at both sides of the situation, rather than blindly cursing someone else. In that situation the curse will surely rebound on you! Examine why there is a difficulty and see whether a simple change in your reaction will solve it. Maybe you need to find a new relationship with the person in which the anger can be dissipated. Magic can help you to change your attitude to the situation; it cannot and must not be used to try to reshape another person or alter her actions. You could assist the person you dislike to find a new job or new home, which will take her out of your orbit and make her happy. If she is gaining a new life, so will you, and there can be no kick-backs. If you try to order angels, powers or people about to suit your own purposes, you will build up a lot of grief for yourself. Selfishness is a harmful attitude.

Affairs of the heart are the most widely given reasons for wanting to interfere in the lives of others. You may want to get rid of an old love, get back an old love, find a new love or discover in which direction your desires really lie. The one thing you have to recognize is that magic may not be used to alter any aspect of anyone else without precise permission. This applies to healing and it certainly applies to love. If you have lost a lover, you must ask yourself, 'In what way did I fail to meet her needs/passions?' The fault lies with you. If you admit to it, then you can change it and maybe get your lover back by allowing her to see the 'new' you. If you are trying to end a relationship, again, honesty is the best policy. If you can't bring yourself to speak what is in your heart, a letter or card, clearly stating how you feel and why you can no longer support the relationship, is by far the safest and best way of dealing with these painful matters.

If you want to attract a new partner or, better still, seek out someone with whom you can share the rest of your life in wedded or hand-fasted bliss, you need to look very hard at yourself. You need to assess your physical attractions, or lack of them (even smelly feet can end the most deliriously happy partnership), and deal with any problems. It is your body and no one else can fix it. If you are overweight, consider why. But both large and small people can make loving and trusted partners, so long as they are happy with who they are. Beauty is in the heart of the beholder. You have to be really honest with yourself and decide what you want from any future partnership. Do you want a slave who will skivvy for you night and day? Do you want a doormat to walk on? Or are you one yourself? Do you offer your own skills at cooking, cleaning and all the little domestic chores which, when equitably shared, make love a joy?

Once you have looked at all the personal details, you can decide what to do about finding a lover. For example, if you don't meet many people in the run of daily life, then perhaps your magical interests could put you in touch with others. There are a number of national and international pagan organizations (listed at the back of magazines, with helpful addresses etc.) and these often have local groups, branches and gatherings. There are also a number of annual conferences and festivals to which outsiders may get tickets. These allow hundreds of people, some alone, to hear speakers, make new friends or participate in workshops and so on. In the USA there are outdoor gatherings as well as regional conferences.

Once you have had an in-depth and truthful look at yourself and then taken steps accordingly, if you decide to add a ritual, you need to consider the following ideas.

Magic works! It can work even if it is badly done by a fumbling amateur. For this reason you must be aware that thoughtless actions or careless words as requests or oaths can get you into trouble. Innocence is no excuse. If you ask for something you may very well get it, along with any on-going consequences this causes! Learn to make your rituals simple, open and exact, and be sure you take account of what will happen after you have got whatever it was you wanted.

Magic also costs! It might be something simple, like a solid gold talisman, dedicated to the Sun to aid a healing; it might be the kind of spell which has to be repeated at sunrise and sunset for a whole Moon, to increase your inner awareness; or it might be that you make a personal life-long dedication, even in a light-hearted moment, and that dedication *will* be life-long and there is nothing you can do to cancel it.

To get rituals to work you have to know how to call upon various sorts of inner plane entities, be they ancient gods and goddesses, angels, spirits or invisible teachers. All have their proper mode of address, all have their own symbols, for these form the language, discovered in meditations, by which they can communicate with you. They are not likely to send you a fax or turn up on e-mail! You need to define your objective very clearly, so that you get what you want without problems attached. Also you need to know how to design the actual ritual, from start to finish, and collect whatever materials, robes, symbols, colours, candles, music and other people you need before you start. Finally, you should be very sure who the deities or other powers are that you are inviting to give inner force to your ritual. It is easy to look up some exotic-sounding name which you cannot even pronounce and later find out it is the Angel of Disasters you have called upon! It really does matter whom you call upon to help you with your magical rituals and spells, so always find out who the god or goddess or angel, whose name is often given in Hebrew, the magical language of the Qabalah, really is. If the book you are using doesn't tell you, look elsewhere. Magic requires effort and study. If you don't know what sort of power to call upon by name, make up an accurate title, like Angel of Peace, Power of Compassion or whatever is necessary. You will find if you study their names that many of the gods and goddesses actually have titles, for example Isis, the Great Goddess of Egyptian magic, has a name, 'Aset', which means 'Throne'.

A Simple Ritual of Dedication

In order to work any ritual successfully you will need to be very organized and this first ritual exercise involves the preparation of an altar. This can be any level surface – a small table, the top of a bookcase or the mantelpiece. It will require a clean white cloth cover, two candlesticks and white candles, a goblet of spring water and a dish of salt. Prepare these items and place them aesthetically before you.

Once again enter into your meditative state, sitting in a chair before your altar. Relax and, with your eyes closed, conjure up a picture of your altar and the things on it until it is absolutely clear and real. Imagine that you can float over it, seeing it from other angles. Are you happy with what you have done or is there a stain on the cloth or salt spilled from the dish? When you are sure that everything is as good as you can make it, open your eyes and compare the inner vision with what you can see before you.

Now you are ready to begin a first ritual which will dedicate the items on your altar. As you go on you will need to use a similar ritual to make magic all the things you use or wear or divine with when you learn how.

Light the two candles, left then right, allowing each to flame steadily before going on to the other. Put the used match away from the altar. Look at the flames and become aware that they represent the power of Light which is behind all true magic. Because there are two, they represent the symbolism of polarity, north and south, day and night, god and goddess, and a thousand other pairs of important twin concepts. Imagine the Light spreading from the candles and engulfing you and the rest of the altar. Feel its warmth, sense its movement and energy, discover its power to bless, heal and drive away doubt.

This is the first real experience of magical ritual, knowing that the Light is a real, living force which can affect you and all that it shines upon. This is enough to get the first feeling of magical power, so go no further than this exercise until you can really appreciate the power of Light. Pinch out the candles, right and left, or use a snuffer. It is not proper to blow out magical candles. Some have to be left to burn out completely, others may be snuffed and used again for similar work.

Exercise Fourteen

A Blessing Ritual

Again, light your new candles set out on your altar. Feel the power of the Light flowing through you for a few moments and once again see the image of the altar. Are the altar and its equipment perfect?

This time take the goblet of water and hold it between the candles. Imagine the Light shining through it, making it a special and sacred substance. When you are sure this has happened, dip your first two fingers into the water and touch it to your forehead. You should feel something other than a cold drop of water. Try until you do.

When that has happened and you know the water is special, sprinkle, with the same fingers, a few drops on the altar cover. Again imagine it being lit up with an inner Light and becoming very special. (Anything which you have blessed in this way should always be treated with respect and kept separate.)

Next pick up the dish of salt, hold it between the lighted candles until it, too, fills with Light. It can be sprinkled on your head so that you can test how it feels. Once you are certain it is holy, again drop a few grains on to the altar cloth and on the candlesticks to bless them for all future work. Snuff out the candles and give thanks.

Which Element has been left out? Find a way to make that holy, and to bless your working altar and its equipment. Put everything away in a box or cabinet.

Self-Blessing

Most rituals have a form of self blessing at the beginning, the most common being the sign of a cross. This is far older than Christianity, and is traditionally a symbol of unity and balance.

With your right hand, fingers outstretched, reach above your head and pull down a beam of light. See it clearly in your inner vision. Bring it down to your solar plexus. Then reach out to your right and pull in energy and throw it across your body to the left. Imagine a great ball of light surrounding you in all directions. Put your hands together and draw that holy Light into your own heart, so that you, for the time being, become holy.

Use this exercise at the start and finish of every meditation, from now on, and see the difference. You can make up some words to say with each part of the gesture. The Hebrew words used by Qabalists are 'Ateh Malkuth, ve Geburah, ve Gedulah, Le olahm, Amen.' This means 'Thou art the Kingdom, the Power and the Glory, for ever' and it is a request to the Most High to bless you, the individual, with those kinds of powers for the duration of the ritual or other work.

Chapter Six
In Search of Deity

'As the process of representing the Gods evolved, an individual or group of individuals, as much like the deity as possible, came to represent the Divine by playing the part of the deity.'

Naomi Ozaniec, *Daughter of the Goddess*

In order to work magic you have to accept that there is some kind of power out there which can make your spell work. Without that basic assumption you are making useless invocations and speaking meaningless words. One of the first concepts you will have to grasp, if you are to bring magic into your everyday life, is that from time immemorial there have been gods, goddesses, powers, angels and other worldly beings of immense size or energy, who by supplication, prayer, spells and invocations can be called upon by human beings for assistance, healing, guidance and much more.

Every evolving civilization has had its deities, its temples and its dedicated priesthood to mediate between the gods and the people. A great deal of the literature on magic and other aspects of occultism has much to say about the rites of ancient Egypt, the religions of the ancient world in Greece and Rome, the nature of the Celtic gods, and the power of runic spells. Always there is a harking back to older faiths and beliefs, because we have lost much of the magic from modern, orthodox religions.

In the past the priestesses were healers, oracles, guides and comforters. The priests made the offerings, talked to the gods and heroes, called upon them for success in battle or in commerce. The temple was a place or refuge, of learning, of music and power, but the modern priesthoods have given up their healing arts, have ceased to speak with the voices of their deity, have lost the gift of sympathy and care for their community. Certainly there are exceptions in many places, but today we seldom turn to the Church or its priests for solace. In fact, many people are declaring themselves to be 'pagans' and seeking a new communion with the ancient gods and goddesses of the land or of history.

Originally the pagans were the country folk set apart from the town dwellers. It was in towns and cities that the organized religions like Christianity took root, and the country people who still worshipped trees and wells were looked upon as old-fashioned country bumpkins, or pagans. Today the Pagan Federation, an organization for all who seek to follow that path, has thousands of members in Britain, and there are many similar organizations in the USA and in Europe. What modern pagans are seeking is a faith without book-bound dogma, a religion which honours both women and men in its priesthood, where joy, dance and song form part of the celebrations and where the sacred inner skills of individuals can be developed and made use of. This longing for the return of magic and mystery, for a house-based religion, where divination and guidance are seen as valid aspects of the belief has brought many to read about the old ways.

What orthodox religions seem to have done is to have thrown out the sense of wonder and awe along with the ritual in Latin or the practice of divine guidance. Modern pagans have sought to balance the need for God the Father with Goddess the Mother, and Holy Child, our own kin. Many ancient forms of religion worshipped the female aspect of deity as the life giver, the preserver, the nourisher and the carer, rather than the male ruler, commander and warrior, acting with authority and discipline. The revelation of 'Gentle Jesus, meek and mild...' offered none of the mother loving which the older goddesses showed.

Pagans are able to accept the idea of reincarnation and the laws of karma, which, roughly translated, means that both the cause and the effect are on the head of the doer. If you live many times, you will pay for your own errors, make good your failings, or suffer the consequences for your own, eternal spirit. You don't need any other to die for your sins – you die for your own and are reborn to come back to put right those parts of your lives where you went wrong.

Many people have had first-hand experiences of their own past lives, brought about through dream, meditation or by the careful use of hypnosis. Once these memories have been evoked, they often change the whole outlook of a person's life. If you can sense that dying is a brief episode in a long line of eternal evolution, then it has less of a sting. If you know you will live many times, then you can accept the death of those you love, because you know that they, too, will live again and that you may meet to continue your relationship. In nature, trees do not die each winter, they cast their leaves to be renewed in spring. Humanity does the same and, at the end of a life cycle, casts off the body from the eternal self and rests in some other world, often seen as a garden by those who have clinically died and been brought back to life. In due course, a new life is planned, choices made and the soul returns to incarnation as a baby, to fulfil its destiny.

This sense of eternal life is a way of recognizing that each of us is an individual and everlasting soul which has a purpose to discover through many lifetimes. We start to realize that there is something beyond the material world and that the short span of each life shows us the next step. A lot of people seek spiritual guidance, not necessarily through the Spiritualist Church, with its mediums and messages from the departed, but by making a personal connection with the realms beyond. In the past the great faiths set the moral standards, on family life, on food, on prayer and religious observances, but today in the West people have turned away from these, casting aside the religious teachings and the moral guidance that goes with it. No longer are the commandments 'Thou shalt not kill, thou shalt not steal, thou shalt not have any other gods before me, honour thy father and thy mother' part of our ethical code. Look at the result! Youngsters are lost in a sad maze of desire for material things or for the mental escape from the world by the use of drugs. In either case they lose their own self-respect and respect for other people and their belongings.

Others who have gone part way down this path have found alternatives. Often they have had some sort of experience which has changed their lives and then they have looked for a new spiritual direction. This is most often found in either an extremely fundamentalist Church or in some form of paganism. Pagans will try to put all individuals in touch with the god and goddess of their tradition. This is a path of personal knowledge, not implied dogma. By meditation and other forms of magical or ritual dedication it is possible to gain direct communication, healing and guidance from the deities themselves. This is not an act of belief, but of personal experience. The pagan creed does not say 'Do as I tell you' but 'Try this exercise and see for yourself!'

The value of a spiritual understanding is basically that there is more to life than gaining a whole lot of *things*. What you gather in one lifetime may well be lost in the next, but what you gain in spiritual insight, wisdom, beneficial powers, such as those which may be gained through magical work, can go with you from life to life. It is the skill to make music from a previous life which shows up child prodigies, or the ability to heal or to see into the future, learned in the ancient temples in the past. As we each evolve, the whole human race takes a small step forwards. If humanity fails its heritage, we will all sink back and life will become intolerable.

To gain spiritual insights often requires some dramatic event to happen first. People who have survived accidents or life-threatening situations often seem to show a new spiritual direction. Having had their lives returned to them they then feel the need to make something of that prize. In near-death experiences, growing even more common due to the advances in medical expertise and high-speed response to crises, many survivors share a common vision. They see themselves moving through a dark tunnel towards a bright light. When they emerge into this brilliance they are often in a paradise-like garden and find figures coming to greet them. Sometimes these are family members or friends who have already died, or they may be shining images of Jesus or an angel or another religious being. There seems to be an overwhelming feeling of love, harmony and peace. Yet, for those who return to life, there is a powerful pull to return to their battered bodies, to go back to complete the duties of that life.

Other people undergo a 'peak experience', as described by Colin Wilson, where during a moment of love or fear or danger, they find they are seeing themselves from outside their bodies, proving that the spirit is separate, and can separate, and can endure from life to life. This helps individuals to see that there are dimensions of experience which go far beyond their previous feelings. There dawns a sense of eternity and the need to do something of lasting worth. Some of them have seen God or the gods of the ancients and it changes their lives.

The need to acknowledge that there are powers beyond ordinary human activities and that forces, unseen in daily life, can be called upon to help us may be difficult to grasp. But once you have been able to accept, if not yet to experience, these beings, you can call to your assistance enormous forces. The very force of life is a reality, turning the dead matter of the newborn universe into a place full of many forms of life – plants, animals, trees and people.

From the birth of the cosmos many forms of living beings have evolved. Not all of them are visible, for example angels, the robots of the Most High, created to serve, to act as messengers and to help other forms of being when they are asked. Each individual has a Holy Guardian Angel from her first birth until the time she has evolved to the greatest height and leaves earthly existence forever. Our angel is always with us, hidden only by our normal ignorance. These angels appear in dreams, not always in the form of a shining, human-like figure with wings, but as guardian animals, friendly creatures or guiding birds. In times of great stress their hands can be felt, bringing calm and inner strength. In the past, magicians used lengthy purification ceremonies, continued for six months, using prayer, offerings of incense and individual devotion, to bring them sight of their Holy Guardian Angel. Today these same rituals are performed with similar results, although magic has progressed and simpler and more direct ways of communicating with your Holy Guardian Angel are possible.

You may not personally have any feeling about a god of any sort, but if you want your rituals to have any power, you must recognize that to create anything takes two parts. Every child has two genetic parents, every seed requires ovum and pollen to fertilize it. To make magic work you need both your own personal input, be it practical, mental or spiritual, and assistance from the inner powers. You don't need to believe in them, but they are real and are essential to any spell being effective. In time, if you are able to try out rituals, you will gradually become aware of other forces, energies, patterns of light or changes in your own way of seeing the world, and then you will know the invisible powers of creation are working with you, to accomplish your aim.

In the past the earliest supernatural powers were attributed to natural things, perhaps strange boulders of rock found in the landscape, whose curved surface resembled a pregnant female; perhaps a rare tree, offering shade or fruit or useful wood. Springs of water were thought to be magical, with healing powers or the ability to show the future in their dark waters. Caves were the dwelling-places of powerful wild animals – wolves and bears and large cats – and these beasts were thought to be allies of spiritual powers. When early people first made their homes in caves, the wild creatures lived near them or had to be driven out with fire. Even fire was thought to be a magical substance, brought down from the sky as a flash of lightning to a tree. From that scarce source new flames were caught and guarded. Fire was used to change food by cooking, change ore into metal and eventually to produce our everyday magical power today, by driving stream turbines, be they coal, oil or nuclear fuelled. Electricity has changed our lives and we would find it hard to live without it. All this came from early reverence of a natural force.

Reverence and thanksgiving are two forms of ritual used today by magicians and witches. There are always things to give thanks for and it is important to acknowledge this. In everyday life there are sudden moments of joy, brought on by seeing the sunlight dancing on water or the cries of a newborn child or success in some project. At that moment a quiet 'thank you' may work wonders and set in train a number of other happy events. Sometimes you may find yourself in a place of outstanding beauty, in a wood or by the sea or in a cultivated garden. Suddenly, for a moment only, the place feels like paradise and you have an overwhelming sensation of one-ness with everything. It is at moments like these that you experience a real sense of reverence and such feelings cannot be made to happen to order.

You will need to think hard about your own concept of deity. Do you have a childhood memory of religious instruction or have you sought some kind of gods for yourself ? Do you believe in 'God the Father' as a stern heavenly parent or do you have other, definable images of what you think God would be like? Do you feel closer to the idea of a vast force, without shape or form, certainly not a human-type shape? Can you see, with inner sight, great moving swathes of coloured lights sweeping the sky or smaller balls of dancing brilliance within your room? Each of these could be an angelic force or an elemental energy.

In magic you will soon discover that no matter what your personal concept of deity might be, if you sincerely ask for help, something will come to your aid. You don't need to see human-like forms of gods and goddesses standing guard at the quarters of your circle, nor do you have to force images of these super-human beings into your imagination. Certainly the gods are real, but they are *not people*. Their forms and appearances, like those of angels, are adapted to our human view, so that they appear to us in vision as the classical sculptors shaped them or the medieval artist painted them. What they are truly like to them-selves you will have to discover for yourself, by gently inviting them to appear to you. Ask that they come in a form you can recognize and in a way which will not terrify you. They are often spoken of in witch ritual as the 'vast and mighty ones', and so they are. They are genuinely awesome, but they are still willing to manifest themselves to the sight of those who will take men-tal steps in their direction. By entering the silence and the stillness of mind, it becomes possible to see these gods in human-like shape, talk to them as you would with old friends and ask for help or power.

Unless you are able to have these experiences, knowing in your heart that there really are powers who can assist you, work-ing in harmony with your own will to achieve whatever is your aim, then your magic won't work and doing it is a waste of time. Learn to know that together with your own eternal spirit there are forces in our everyday world, unseen and usually unfelt, that can turn the spell you make into part of the future. In magic this should not be a matter of belief, but of knowledge and experi-ence. If you need to see the old gods, ask them to come, but be prepared for them to show themselves. Once you have devel-oped this awareness of beings from other realms of creation, you will become certain that they can help with your magic and add greater dimension to your experience of the world.

Most people are used to having birthday parties and celebra-tions at Christmas or similar public festivals, but in most calen-dars of the old gods there are many such occasions where a feast or remembrance takes place. In the modern pagan calendar there are eight times of year when Nature or the Sun shows it is a proper time for celebration and in older folk traditions there may be far more sacred seasons. Some groups of natural magicians who work with the phases of the Moon have 12 or 13 gatherings each year, while others who work with both the new and full Moons have twice that number. Just as there are saints' days in the Christian calendar, so there are special dates to commemorate all sorts of other teachers and anniversaries of the classical gods and goddesses. There are many good books which detail what makes every day in the year special, either as a landmark in the agricultural cycle of the year or as the epiphany of a god at a particular place. As your knowledge grows in whichever tradition you choose to follow, you will learn the importance of certain times of year. In everyday life you will find time to take into your heart the feelings of the celebration of the coming of spring or of the rising in the sky of the star Sirius, sacred to the ancient Egyptians for it announced the rising of the waters of the Nile. In time these festivals will become woven into your own year and the appropriate way of marking each will give you pleasure. Perhaps you will have a special meal or set out an altar with seasonal symbols, perhaps you will gather with a coven to celebrate Beltane or with a lodge to mark the midsummer solstice. Every day is a festival for some reason or other.

Some rituals you may wish to perform are concerned with seeing into the future by the use of divination. Many students of the occult become expert at reading the symbols of the Tarot cards or the Chinese Book of Changes, the *I Ching*. Today there are dozens of different Tarot packs with images drawn from every possible tradition, Arthurian, Egyptian, Norse, Greek, Aztec and Eskimo, so if you follow one of these paths, you are sure to be able to find a set of images which resonate with you. To use divination in a ritual way ensures that the interpretation is much clearer, for the sealing of a circle and the calming of the mind through meditation helps the cards to speak clearly. Within a quiet place, in a circle made by magic, the story the cards tell will be both deeper in meaning and easier to understand, because all the clatter of mental background noise is shut out. The concentration which regular meditation produces makes all forms of divination far more powerful than they would be at, say, a public festival. Another way which can reveal to you the nearness of the old gods is through an oracle and you may find you hear their voices or feel their touch during a ritual divination. Their pictures may step out of the cards into your circle, once you know how to invite them.

You may wish to ask certain deities to protect you, or your home, or your car, so you need to know which can be called upon for this task. To protect yourself from the mental disturbance of the unkind thoughts of others it is best to ask your Holy Guardian Angel to look after you. As you saw earlier in this book, there is a way of making a circle of calmness about you, so do that and then ask your angel to be with you during the time of need. This is not meant to be a permanent protection, just for the time you feel yourself to be at hazard. If you set up full-time protection you will become isolated and lonely, for the circle which protects you also cuts you off from the feelings and friendship of others. All traditions of gods have one who is concerned with guardianship, for example Anubis, the jackal-headed god from Egypt, is often called upon to act as an invisible guard dog by those who work with that tradition. Or you could call upon the help of the spirit of one of King Arthur's knights to protect you. Study the various pantheons of god and goddesses and see who can be of use.

If you make yourself open to the possibility of seeing the many ancient gods and goddesses, and imagine the places they might inhabit, the symbols with which they are associated and the way in which their help can be invited, you will come to know these great beings. Once you know them you can offer them thanks, burn symbolic items as incense in honour of them, celebrate their special dates with a party or in many other ways. They can become unseen but readily available friends, to call on when you are lonely or in need of support. By saying 'thank you' now and again, you will receive confirmation of their abilities to help you.

If in time you become a member of a lodge or coven, there

are other ways in which you might encounter the gods. Most covens have sets of named goddesses and gods whom they call upon during their rituals. In some covens the High Priestess calls the Goddess to enter her so that she can become the voice of the Lady, or the High Priest may become overshadowed by one of the gods. In this way these mighty beings can be present within the hallowed circle, during the rite. Many call upon this to happen, but it doesn't always occur. You have to be prepared to be changed during the process and unless you have had a lot of practice at meditation, so that you can become receptive to inner voices, it won't work. In very rare cases the priestess or priest is really altered in looks, words and behaviour to become an aspect of the deity. They themselves are unaware of what is happening, having totally surrendered themselves to become the mouthpiece of the gods.

In ceremonial magic there is a similar process, which has seldom been written about. During a particular kind of ritual, when guidance is sought from an inner teacher or inner plane adept one of the most senior initiates in the lodge may put herself into an altered state of consciousness whereby the teacher can speak through her. This differs greatly from both Spiritualist mediums' work and that of modern 'channellers' in that the receiver of guidance is aware of what is happening. It is a kind of spiritual partnership whereby the advanced rituals of many occult orders, including the famous Hermetic Order of the Golden Dawn at the end of the nineteenth century, are brought into being. With this process it is essential that records on tape or paper are kept of what is said, so that all practical teachings can be put into use.

As a novice at the various magical arts, you will only need to learn that there are many gods and goddesses whom you can call upon, that there are angels who have your personal welfare as their primary task, and that other invisible powers can be summoned to help you, once you have discovered the keys which call them to you. As you spend more time in meditation you will begin to sense that other presences are near you and that answers to questions can appear. In the stillness and silence of your mind you will discover the images of symbols, the patterns of colour and light in which form many inner beings appear. Once you can see or sense them, you can enter into conversation with them.

It is not necessary to believe in God, in the Christian sense, but to become aware of some being or process which set the cosmos into existence, a Creator, and, nearer to our perception, of layers of other angels and the variety of ancient gods and goddesses. These may be thought of as just symbols which resonate with some of our own inner spiritual levels to form creative and healing partnerships, or they may be known as real living entities in some other dimension of time and space. It is for you to discover how you feel.

You need to consider whatever faith you were raised in. Which parts of it did you enjoy, feel moved by or actively dislike? Can you understand what pleasures other people get out of going to their place of worship? Have you had any experience of the new pagan movement or sought to worship the old gods for yourself? If you don't have any spiritual beliefs or feelings, you will find it very hard to get magic to work. You need to see yourself, with all humanity, as an eternal spirit wrapped in a mortal body, capable of evolution and having a purpose in earthly life. The more you are able to accept this idea, the easier you will find it to participate fully in any pagan or orthodox religious rituals. What you do and believe has to have real meaning for you, otherwise it is a waste of time.

All religions have had their creation myths, the stories of the coming of mankind, the development of civilization and the ways in which the ancient people made contact with their gods. We know that the world developed from a sterile ball of matter, long after the 'Big Bang' which, scientists explain, caused everything to come into being. Everything has changed and evolved, so *something* had to set that process in motion. If some power can cause change, which in due time advanced into the life we find all around us, then that power and its offspring can be called upon to perform the willed changes we call magic. Plants grow from seeds, adults grow from babies, success grows from failure, each in its own way. By understanding the forces which have always been there, to change war to peace, sickness to health, winter to summer, we can learn to make contact with them, ask them for help and predict the results.

Today new pagan priesthoods are springing up, bringing a new kind of self-knowing religion to people in many parts of the world. These new priests and priestesses will have to take up the many-faceted roles that their ancient predecessors held. We need spiritual guidance, we need healing of body, mind and spirit, we need to find officiants for our naming ceremonies, marriages and burial rites. We need oracles to teach us the words of the gods direct and we need diviners who can accurately read the symbols which can guide us through our everyday lives. We need interpreters of dreams and visions and teachers of the right ways, for us, to celebrate the sacred seasons. We need initiates, who can, when we are ready, lead us through the rituals of initiation and the magical grades which show to the world the skills we have gained. These duties have always been the professions of those within the Mysteries, those experiential ways of gaining information and wisdom which are hidden in the light of day. We need expounders of secret knowledge, whose silence we respect, and whose teaching we will take with clean hands and a pure heart, and whose sacred knowledge we will only share within the magical circle.

All these professions are being relearned and new generations are springing up to fill the spiritual needs of those people to whom the New Age, the Age of Aquarius, is an era of spiritual growth. There are no formal schools or seminaries in which pagan priests and priestesses can gain their training but the world of daily life. There is much inner work, study, meditation and prayer which prepares these new spiritual guides before they can help others. They do not need churches, for their deities are too large to fit into buildings and too free to be confined. The Great Ones are out there, all around us, but invisible.

The way to meet them is in silence and with an open heart. Ask for help and in dreams or mediation you will receive it. Look for teachers and when you are really ready for their instruction, you will find them. If you want to meet the old gods, find out where their dwelling-place is and conjure it in your own magical circle. When the time is right, you will meet them face to face.

Exercise Sixteen

Building the Temple

In many ancient traditions there is the idea of the 'Temple not made with hands'. This is a powerful image which has to be conjured into existence by mental effort rather than brick-laying.

To begin, relax and calm yourself in the way of other meditations. See before you a dark landscape under a starry sky. Imagine it with as much clarity as you can manage. If you can't see it, feel the atmosphere of a warm night, smell the scented wild flowers and incense-laden shrubs of a Mediterranean hillside. Gradually see day dawning, when the sky pales and turns from indigo to peach and then to clear azure blue. See a sloping landscape with dark bushes, reddish earth, scattered wild flowers in brilliant reds and yellows, and, not too far away, a small white classical temple, with six pillars supporting the triangular portico. Feel the heat, and smell the flowers and the dust.

Walk, in your imagination, towards the steps of the temple. Climb them slowly and enter the cool shade of the porch. Look at the white marble floor, the fluted, slender columns and the door of dark bronze, standing open to the darkness within. Enter the cool and dark temple, and allow the images of what is within, or the feelings such a sacred place invokes, to flow over you. Begin to see a shape looming out of the darkness, a vast, human-like form of one of the classical deities. Feel a sense of awe and wonder.

When the figure has come close, see what it looks like, how

it is dressed, and what feelings its presence arises within you. Talk to it and see how the answers appear, within your own mind or as a voice from beyond the silence.

(To get the full benefit from this kind of exercise you will either need to get a friend to slowly read the description to you or record it and play it back, leaving pauses between the sentences. Otherwise you will have to learn each section, image by image, and run through them as you sit poised and relaxed with your eyes closed.)

Other pictures, words and feelings may well come to you, so note them down. When you have finished this, stamp your foot on the ground three times to mark the conclusion. This is important, as it prevents inner material overflowing or meditation images impinging at times when it is inappropriate. With all magical acts, you must know you are in total control.

Exercise Seventeen

Seeking the Wilderness Powers

This is another 'inner journey'. You should work at each section until it becomes clear in feeling, sight or sensation. Gradually work through these images and again see what sorts of beings approach you, how you feel when talking to them and what else you experience.

Imagine yourself walking along a path in the countryside on a warm summer day. At first you are walking across hay meadows full of wild flowers and tall grasses. Beyond them the land rises and there is the edge of a wood. It stretches along the whole horizon and the path you walk vanishes into it. You step into the shade under the trees and see that the path winds onwards and upwards. The trees are familiar to you, rich with green leaves this summer day. Twining vines have sweet flowers and at your feet there are mosses and wild flowers. In the undergrowth you sense the movement of wild animals and above you the songs of birds echo in the leafy canopy. You feel at peace, for this is an ancient and untouched forest, and the path you follow was made by deer.

The tall trees stand far enough apart for you to see a long way, but you are shaded by the spreading branches and can see only leaves above you. Time passes as you wander onwards and a sense of sacredness begins to creep over you. Apart from the sounds of birds and movements of the leaves it is very quiet, and you become aware how safe and calm you feel. Gradually you begin to sense you are no longer alone and a large form seems to emerge from a patch of deep shadow. Could it be a large animal, a tall person or a being of the Wildwood? You do not know, but you still feel secure. The shadow comes towards you and your steps slow to watch. Here is one of the great beings of the wild, the ruler of the ancient forest, and gradually you being to see the details. Is it an animal or human shape? Is it male or female? Is it friendly or threatening or just really awesome? You will see as you open your inner sight. Pause for a while, coming to terms with what you are encountering.

After a while, begin to ask questions and wait silently for answers, again, either within your mind or as a voice or in some other way. Be patient.

Eventually the light within the Wildwood fades and the figure merges back into the gloaming. Around you the birdsong rises to its evening chorus and the leaves rustle as the wind stirs the branches. Before you the path that brought you here is clear in the falling twilight, pale against the darker forest loam. You offer thanks for whatever experience, great or small, has befallen you and make your way swiftly from the woodland shade to the brighter evening light on the meadows. Here the small flowers have closed for the night and the grasses wave in the breeze. As you walk across the meadow, the image fades, but the memory of what you have seen and felt remains clear in your mind. Gently you return to your normal waking state. Be prepared to jot down some of the appearances in your vision, before, like dreams, they fade.

Each of these last two exercises can be repeated many times and on every occasion you, and perhaps your friends, will have new experiences, and see clearer and deeper visions. Inner journeying is an ancient art, like story-telling, which awakens in most people the power of inner sight or senses.

Exercise Eighteen

The Stairway to Heaven

Once again, relax, close your eyes and become still and inwardly focused. Feel yourself to be in an open air place, high up, under a starry night sky. Become aware that you are standing on the top of a high plateau where a gentle wind is blowing. See above you a moonless sky, but one filled with stars in many colours, sparkling light tiny jewels strewn across black velvet. Feel the distance and the nearness of them. Turn round slowly, seeing and sensing the vast spaces, the sense of alone-ness and the immense numbers of stars above you.

As you turn around you see that a long staircase of glass-like crystal stretches from near your feet up towards the stars. You begin to climb, finding the effort small, as if you are weightless. Swiftly you rise up and before you a huge cluster of stars seems to outline a doorway of sky. The steps take you straight to that starry door, and you reach out and feel another crystalline panel covered with stars, which moves at your touch. You open the door and see beyond a circular room with glassy walls and glowing brilliance. It feels safe and secure and warm.

You enter into this otherworldly place, feeling light and joyful. Standing there to greet you is a great angelic form. Dressed in silky opalescent robes, the angel moves to meet you, and a sense of blessing and peace comes over you. Here is a real angel, one of the Shining Ones, whose realm is between the Earth and the stars, and you are there to receive healing or wisdom or benediction. Again you enter into communion, in words, feelings or sensations, taking your time with the questions and waiting until answers are received.

Time will pass and you may find different emotions flowing over you. Here you are in the region above the Moon, where joy and sorrow, laughter and pain and all other feelings have their being. Allow yourself to experience whatever this angelic sphere has to offer. When you are ready, again give heart-felt thanks to the angel, ask a blessing upon your life and return through the starry doors. Before you the stairs lead safely and gently back to Earth. Bring with you the sense of harmony, power and light which you have received.

Return fully to your ordinary waking state and remember to write down details of your experience.

This and the earlier exercises may all be repeated, not too often, as you feel the need of them. Each will always reward you with new insights, feelings or visions.

Chapter Seven
The Enchanted Forest

'Dark forests, and remote castles...and in the yellow, sunlit glades, there were always strange treasures to be found...'

Robert Holdstock, *Lavondyss*

There are many different sorts of magic which you can learn and make part of your everyday life, but it might help you to know a little about the various possibilities.

A first choice is whether you wish to work alone or whether you seek the companionship of a group, lodge or coven. Only you can decide and from that initial choice, further choices will spring. Although you may decide to join a group, you still have to find one, and convince those in charge of it you are worthy and willing to become a part of their group mind in due course. Places in all occult groups worth their salt have to be won by effort. If you meet someone in a pub, chat about witchcraft or spells for a while and then that stranger asks you to turn up next Wednesday with a bottle of red wine and a fat cheque to some unknown address when you will be initiated, turn away quickly.

There are two levels of inner knowledge, known as the Lesser Mysteries and the Greater Mysteries. The Lesser Mysteries are the outer aspects of secret knowledge which can be found in books. They are things which can be talked about, explained and learned by taking in and using that open knowledge. The Greater Mysteries can only be gained after a fair understanding of the Lesser Mysteries has been achieved, because the Great Mysteries can only be understood by revelation. You cannot be told about them, understand them or become part of them from the outside, you have to enter in, have a personal experience and then they will be made clear. To the outsider there will be nothing you can say. The initiates of the Mysteries of Eleusis were given an ear of wheat as a symbol of the Greater Mysteries which they had experienced. To everyone else that was just an ear of wheat, but to the initiate it had great significance.

Every land and tradition had its own Mysteries and trained priests and magicians, both men and women, to make contact with the gods and show the people the power of their deities through festivals, rituals and dramas. Sometimes these Mystery Traditions lasted for thousands of years. Even Christianity has its Mysteries: when the priest raises the consecrated host it becomes symbolically the flesh of the Risen Christ. The people just see the wafer of bread, while the initiated priest of the tradition sees the transubstantiated substance. The Western Mystery Tradition acknowledges the power of the Christian faith, but sees it as one more turn in the spiral of evolution which takes human spirits and changes them into divine forms.

One symbol which links both the Christian and pre-Christian Mysteries is the Holy Grail. In the Christian story the cup that was used by Jesus at the Last Supper was brought by Joseph of Arimathea to Britain, and with it came a healing power. In the Arthurian legends the Knights of the Round Table set off to seek the Holy Grail, but here it is not always described as a cup or chalice, as it appears as a flat dish or platter, a stone that fell from heaven (perhaps as a meteorite) or a spear which drips blood. Here is a Mystery in our own Western European lands.

In the earliest written versions, in Welsh, the magical container is a great cauldron, which King Arthur and his companions fetch from Annwn, the Otherword, in Arthur's magical ship, Prydwen. He is accompanied by Merlin and Taliesin, a magician and a poet or story-teller. Few of the knights make a safe return and 'None save seven came back from Caer Achren.' The cauldron can not only heal the sick, but any dead person who was put into this vast cooking pot came out alive.

There are many tales of magical cauldrons in Celtic mythology, which tell the outer version of the inner Mysteries. Always these provided life, healing or even the food the individual liked most in the world. Sometimes the cauldron was filled with light, and images of the past, the future and distant lands could be seen in its seething contents. Later on it became closely associated with witches, who were often depicted in fiction stirring strange potions in a big black iron pot over the fire. In real life, the cauldron was every home's only cooking vessel and it provided soup, stew, boiled puddings and hot water for everyday purposes. Today we have electric kettles and central heating boilers which perform the same function. These things are pretty vital to comfortable life!

The stories about King Arthur and his Round Table, the ladies and knights, the Quest and the conquests are all disguised descriptions of the path of the initiate in the Western Mysteries. Each individual has to set off on a personal Quest, a journey of exploration which need not take the seekers out of their own homes. Challenges have to be overcome today, just as much as in the Dark Ages. If you say you have taken up magic, people will ask you to perform card tricks, and if you try to explain what ritual is about you can get asked some very difficult questions. You see your studies and activities as an 'insider', but those without your knowledge or experience may see you as mad and your work as harmful or dangerous. The dragons we have to overcome today are the dark-scaled minds which will not allow the unusual to be real, while the wild forests are the urban jungles in which we live and have our daily round – and they can be just as fearful and unfriendly as the untamed land in the past.

We do not have to know how to handle a sword, for the pen is mightier than the sword and the keyboard mightier yet. We do not have armour and a horse to take us Questing, we have a car which serves both purposes: protection from others who might harm us and a fast means of transport. However, we still need to acknowledge the eternal players in the great drama of the Western Mysteries. There are, as there always have been, magicians like Merlin, a mage who worked alone, a poet, a healer, a military strategist and King Arthur's friend. There are the questing knights, rich and poor, educated and less so, who seek the Holy Grail, whatever it may be, in order that the Wasteland may be made fertile again. There are hermits and guides who solve riddles, give spiritual counsel and provide help to those who get lost. There are powerful ladies, both as Questers in their own right (and Dindraine was a Grail Gainer in her own way) and as sorceresses and herbalists. There are sacred places, both pagan and Christian, there are the Lands Adventurous and the ancient Wildwood, there are castles to explore and deeds to perform. Somewhere in this Mystery there is something for everyone who loves the Earth.

That is the whole point. Achieving the Grail will release the waters and make the Wasteland green again. We don't have to look far to see that much of the Earth is suffering drought or flood, tornado or earthquake, bitter cold or unseasonable heat. Almost every day news is broadcast of yet another natural disaster somewhere. The Wasteland is growing, both on the face of the planet and in the minds of the people. Many have sunk so low through poverty, homelessness, sickness, deprivation or disaster that they have lost hope of things getting better. They have even become so hopeless that they are not able to take advantage of any good which may come their way. This is happening not only in the 'Third World' but in our own fertile and rich lands. Without hope, the most blessed place feels like the Wasteland and so it becomes an attitude of mind as well as the state of the land and its cities.

Humanity is responsible for many of the changes in the state of the world. Pollution from cars far outweighs pollution from factories. Burning petrol in cars, gas in heating and coal for fuel changes the balance of gases in the air and increases carbon dioxide so that the fewer trees can no longer absorb it. If we make the Wasteland green by foresting barren land, by reforesting or preserving at all costs the natural forests in Europe, just as much as in the Amazon basin, and try to cut down on use of chemicals, fuels and processes which continue to add to the burden of pollution, we may succeed. This is also part of our heritage of magic. Magic is an art of the mind, but if the world around us is decaying and diseased, then the more subtle levels of astral light are polluted too. This is one of the reasons why people studying magic now find it harder to concentrate, find it harder to get clear visions or direct guidance. If we work on all levels, practical and magical, mental and spiritual, to clean up the world, the Earth can be healed and the people with her.

It may seem a daunting task for any individual, but there are thousands of others like you, around the world, who worship the Earth Mother as a living and sustaining goddess, as indeed she is, or who revere the ancient gods of the land, celebrate their festivals and honour the old ways. If you join that secret company, every effort you make for healing will be reflected a thousand times from the True Wills of other people. You will become aware in your meditations that currents of healing power are stirring, darkness and decay is being rooted out and delicate new green growth is possible. Even by reading one book you have already stepped off the ordinary path, because you have seen new possibilities, not really of power over others, if you have any common sense, but power from within, which can surely heal and change the world.

New ideas and changed approaches to everyday things will start to bring the magic into your life. It is not necessary to dedicate all your spare time to gaining mastery of these ancient arts, but it is a help! You will often find that you naturally start to change the pattern of your life, turning away from the pub, the cinema and the ordinary pleasures. You may start to actually prefer to be still and quiet and inward looking, for there is the seat of all knowledge and the beginning of wisdom. This is usually a slow, subtle and gentle change, but it can have a profound effect upon your outlook to life.

For example, once you have found that a simple spell actually seems to have worked, the boost in your confidence can be enormous. It can also alter your whole attitude to life, because suddenly you have another tool or strategy to help you. You feel you have a certain amount of power, you have achieved something unexpected. The second spell may not work, or the results may be difficult to understand, but in time you will learn how to make your magic work every time.

There is a kind of magical labyrinth within the Enchanted Forest of mystical knowledge. Each path is a new ritual worked or piece of magic tried. Some lead you towards your own goal of initiation, power or self-awareness, some are dead ends. Gradually you will learn the pattern of paths, but you cannot do it without effort. You have to try walking those inner ways until you understand the maze and what good it can bring you. This is a gradual process. If you have the dedication to work every day at meditation, as the real magicians meditate every day of their lives, the maze will unravel faster.

You may also gain insight into which of the various paths of magic you really want to follow. As already discussed, it is not safe to dip into various books or have odd bits of weekend teaching in different systems and then try to mix a bit of shamanic drumming with Egyptian ritual, or Norse runes in a Tarot divination. Each is separate. For safety's sake, keep it that way. Otherwise you are acting like a mad plumber, running water through gas pipes and trying to get electric power out of water pipes. As you can imagine, the result could be extremely dangerous. Certainly, when you have had years of experience you can change from one system to another safely, but each one is then worked separately on each occasion. Prepare yourself to stick to one system or tradition for at least a year and then try another. You simply have to be patient and work hard or magic will elude you.

Whichever tradition you decide to try first, or next, you will need to be prepared to spend time reading, researching and understanding the legends, history and traditions of that path.

Today, as already mentioned, there are many books detailing various traditions, but sadly, some of them have been based on very flimsy scholarship. Often, because writers want to make the worship of goddesses important, they have attributed names, powers and aspects to them, which they never had in history. The idea that there were always sets of three Moon Goddesses, for example, appears to have been made popular by the poet Robert Graves. Certainly in classical times there were lots of gods and goddesses, and some of these went in threes, but they are not always associated with the Moon.

Many writers are inspired to share with their readers their own personal visions and often they never look back to check whether the ancient people whose rites they are bringing to the modern world would have acted or worshipped as they suggest. Many traditions which came to us in their classical forms, as late as the 1960s and early 70s, have been 'updated' and altered and have wandered far from the original path. There are many ways to look at this recreation of the past and it will be up to you, if you follow the works of contemporary writers, to decide for yourself. Either you are trying to re-establish an ancient tradition in the way it was used by those who made it or you are working on a modern path, invented and set out by the current teachers of that heritage. These are two different things.

One area which gets little mention in these 'be kind to animals' days is that most of the ancient temples were tended by priests who offered animals as sacrifice. If you wanted to attract the attention of Athene or Zeus or Venus, there was a proper offering, of blood, from a bull or goat or bird; doves were sacrificed to Venus to bring true love! If you want to study ancient Egyptian rites, look at the wall paintings of heaps of dead wildfowl, slaughtered cattle and sheep being laid out before the priests, who offered some as a burnt sacrifice to the gods and ate the rest. Honey, wine and flowers as well as birds and beasts were offered. Even the famous quotation from Charles Leland's *Aradia* about being naked in your rites goes on to say that you can use your witchly power to kill your enemies! Those who follow part of this text should look at the rest, the bits about poisoning your enemies, making spells to curse, and charms to bring conflict and death. It is not all sweetness and light, and certainly the old Italian witch who told her story to Leland didn't reveal everything. What I am trying to say is that if you take up part of a tradition you must have the courage to look at all of it, not just the edited highlights which often reach modern books.

The world has changed, but if you choose to walk into the Enchanted Forest, the inner magical land, beware. There are dangers there, there are dark forces which can scare you and grant you sleepless nights. The past was not a Golden Age, but tough and cruel, and the traditions we have inherited were often dark with the blood of sacrificed victims. If you venture into these hidden lands you may become aware of lurking images and feel shadowy presences all around you. Some of these are the ghosts of what has been, recalled to the world by those who want to summon the past glories. Others are parts of your own being, the hidden secrets which you alone know and have tried to conceal. In the light of the Otherworld all secrets may be revealed, and you will have to confront your hidden fears and forgotten failures. The things that lurk in the dark are as much a part of you as your feet or your hair. You cannot banish them any more than you can banish your knees! What you have to do is to confront them, honestly, in the privacy of your meditations. Look them in the face, which is your face, at another time and in another phase, and let them teach you. It is the only way to exorcise these dark shadows, but, like much in real magic, it takes courage. There is nothing so fearful in the inner worlds as your own naked soul, the true self, good and bad, which you have built in your lives on Earth.

Many schools of magic adhere to the concept, written over the door of the Temple at Elusis, 'Know Thyself.' There is no other path which leads safely and surely to the Light than that of honest self-knowledge. It is hard, but it is also a personal task which no one can do for you. You have lived through this life, and perhaps many other lives, accruing karma, that burden of benefit and loss gained through your actions. No one can take it from you, you cannot sell it or buy a respite from the outcome of your own action. You can only learn where you have failed, ignored good advice and come unstuck in your lives. Also, only you have a *right* to that knowledge. There are people who claim to read your past lives from your hand or your horoscope, but they have no right to that knowledge, just as they have no right to know your bank balance, sexual history or anything else about this life, unless you choose to tell them. The gates that guard the Akashic Records are strong and only the true seeker with a clear motive has the right to open them and know what there is to know about their soul's journey.

When you have looked hard at who you are now, how you have arrived there and where you desire to go, in meditation and through self-examination, then you can explore the deep levels of the Enchanted Forest safely. There you can find treasures to bring back to the light of day. Much of what you find will build on your own self-knowledge, for knowledge is power. You will see that you can conquer fears of the Otherworld, you can tread the paths safely to other realms, which are other levels of consciousness. There you will gain skill in perception, the arts of divination and far seeing, the ability to heal and to work with power. These are not gifts of the outer world, but of the hidden regions of inner awareness.

Because we all live in an urban world which has cut back the woods, concreted over the moorlands and driven the country-side back into a fenced and tamed place, it does not mean that the Enchanted Forest of the mind has been obliterated. That wilderness is there for any who seek it and in it can be found all kinds of magical adventures. There you can meet the heroes, the old gods and goddesses of the wild, the lords of the land who are usually invisible, and the ladies of life who empower the seasons. It is a small step, within the quietness of your own place and in the deeps of your own consciousness, to discover the past and progress on your own Quest. Remember that you have a valid way of entering that Otherworld, in search of the way which will best lead you to your personal, magical goal, and that you will find guides there, in the guise of animals, birds or otherworldly beings, or teachers in human form, if you have the courage to look for them. Through meditation you can gain the passwords which will allow you access to the true Wildwood and all its secrets.

In the everyday world you will have to look for magic on your travels. The way is no easier now than it was to battle your way through the unexplored Wildwood of ages past. Nowadays you could start with the library, for example, or the local mind, body and spirit shop. These places, all over the world, contain the essential first clues to every magical path. You will find there written offers of lectures, training, courses and esoteric gatherings in your area. These need to be considered and then followed up. What they will lead to, in due course, will be people! People who have experienced magic, people who know it well enough to teach some of their practical subjects, people who, like you, are Seekers on the path of wisdom, who can help you on your way. Books, on their own, can be helpful, but unless you turn the exercises they suggest into personal experience, they are just so much literature. If you find others on the path you wish to explore, they can share their experiences with you, give warnings, offer practical advice and perhaps go with you on your journey. It can be a very lonely activity and the higher you go the lonelier it will get, but at the start of the journey there are lots of other explorers, lots of beginners seeking the best way.

As you advance on your own way of knowledge, others may ask you for help and advice, and you would be wise to offer to assist as well as you can. There are few fees for the secret knowledge, except to exchange your garnered information with others who share that destination. Often being able simply to talk to someone else can be a great relief. Perhaps you will be fortunate to find on your search of bookshop information boards and the back pages of occult journals exactly the school or coven you are seeking. Often the Quest does not end with one successful find, for eventually you will grow out of that group or study. Just as you moved from level to level at school, maybe going on to college or university, so you will need to progress through different teachers and experiences. Some groups will always be willing to take in beginners, but can only share with them the rudiments of that particular system, and students will have to discover that there can be an end to a settled association with a happy group. Some groups reach a critical mass and explode, due to power battles and interpersonality rows. In the end you may find yourself back on the track through the Wilderness again, but you will be stronger and wiser than before, and so be able to chart a smoother passage through the esoteric maze.

You cannot avoid personality clashes in magical groups because the work tends to make people very sensitive to each other and the world around them. It is often reported by new students of magic that they have the feeling that they are being watched or that they can sense presences around them at night. In one sense what they say is true, but it is their own increased sensitivity, brought on by magical work as simple as meditation, which makes them aware of the many forms of entity which inhabit the world around us. If there has been some sort of trouble within a group due to its natural 'growing pains' and the student starts to become aware of the unseen hovering at the edge of her perception, then she will often start a sort of witch hunt. She may accuse her erstwhile teacher of mentally attacking her or sending out demons to interfere with her life, while really what is happening is that she is becoming aware of the beings, visible to all in dreams, who are living in the same space as her.

When you do start to sense other living things near you, that you may or may not yet be able to see, take it as a good sign, a sign that your inner senses are waking up and becoming available to you. You have the power to control such manifestations, but you must do so each time you make yourself more aware. Every time you sit down to meditate it is worth doing something which makes a ritual of that simple process. You can imagine guardians at the four cardinal points, or light a candle, or even just make the statement out loud that it is your intention to meditate (or whatever). At the end of the exercise be equally, if not more, firm that you are completing the work. When you finish meditation or some other exercise, firmly stamp your foot on the ground or clap your hands to signify the end of that period of open-mindedness. If you don't do this it can lead to psychic intrusions. No matter how brief the meditation may be, always make an effort to begin and end on a formal note. This may not completely stop your feelings of being watched, but it will prevent the state of mind used in meditations from continuing. Gradually, when you can accept that there really aren't evil forces lurking behind every chair or trickling from the pages of some less than helpful book, you will know that you can switch on and off the increased psychic awareness as you need it.

Certainly when you venture into the Otherworld on your inner voyages of discovery you may return feeling somewhat 'spaced out' or distracted, but a firm acknowledgement that you are in the here and now will quell any such feelings. You must learn to be in control of the altered states of consciousness used in magic and set aside any such experiences when you are driving a car or doing ordinary things which require your full attention. Eventually you will find that you can shift from one level to any other at will, completely under control. Then you will know that if you feel eyes on the back of the neck they are probably attached to a very ordinary person who is watching everyone in sight as a cure from boredom!

In time you will become very sensitive to atmospheres in places or any flows of magical energy which are stirred up near to you. These usually appear as swirls of light or rainbow coloured mists or even sparkling fields of energy around people or special objects. Look upon any changes of perception as good signs – after all, you are seeking magical knowledge and it is bound to be different from everyday experience. Gradually you will begin to notice changes in the way you feel about life and the people you meet in it. This will be a confirmation that your regular attempts at inner work are starting to pay dividends. If you only try these exercises in fits and starts, the results may be far less rewarding, as they too will come in lumps, instead of smooth progress. Slowly, your fluency in the language of magic will improve and you will not only be able to focus on your own projects but also be able to sense the responses from the more subtle levels of creation.

Learning magic is very like learning a foreign language and it is best learned in the same way. Either you find a native speaker or, in your case, an experienced magical teacher, or you have to learn from books. Both require continuing practice of dull repetitive exercises which have no immediate reward, both lead to new perceptions of the real world, both can take quite a long time, especially if you are not able to keep on with the initial work. One day, just as you suddenly understand someone who speaks the tongue you are learning, the inner voices of angels or the visions of the gods will come to you. Then you will have made a real breakthrough, received a genuine entry to the Otherworld, on your own, and it will feel great. Hard work in all skills will pay off, but only if you make the commitment and personal effort.

If you are lucky enough to encounter an effective training school or, rarer still, an individual teacher, your progress should be faster. However, the discipline applied by most magical schools is hard, and you will have to submit work regularly, meditate daily and study many other things. The orders of magic are not democratic and all who rise through the grades do so because they have deserved the elevation. It doesn't matter what you may claim as your knowledge, it will be thoroughly tested by practical work, and those who pass the tests will rise higher. It is no good appointing someone as a healer just because lots of people like her, if she fails when healing is needed. Whatever skills you gain will be truly yours and their value will be rewarded. All magical work will eventually pay you dividends in ways that you will appreciate, but they will not be badges you can show to the world.

Some of the paths and traditions you may follow are very ancient, others quite modern inventions, as already mentioned, when today's students learn a little of some older art and then reinterpret it, make it more simple and in many ways deviate from its ancient roots. As you follow your own path you will have to decide how far you are going to go in discovering the real origins of the magical tradition you like best. The one thing you will have in your favour is the fact that by working on the various exercises in magical texts, you will have the skills to ask for help and guidance. In the Bible it says, 'Knock and it shall be opened up to thee, ask and it shall be given...' You really do have to knock or ask for whatever kind of help or guidance you need. The Inner Powers don't wander the land, knocking on doors and trying to sell the occupants magical gifts or enrol them on the path of initiation. You have to seek them out, but they will gladly offer you clues when you ask. The answers are most likely to be extremely ordinary too. You will suddenly notice an invitation to a lecture or that a friend puts you in touch with an initiate. The clues are all round you, but you tend to ignore them because it seems too easy to go to the library and look at the public notice-board, or get a small magazine and check the announcements there for possible steps on your chosen way. Open your eyes – real magic is close at hand and you can have it just for the asking.

Exercise Twenty-one

Seeking a Symbol

This is another mental journey, one to seek out some kind of symbol which the Inner Worlds are offering you. You may well not know what it is to begin with, but if you do some research, in the end you will find it useful. Long ago one of my students shared a guided journey with me and during his vision he saw a strange round object with decorations. Neither of us knew what it was, although he had seen it clearly. We both felt that this was an important symbol for him to discover. In time he did and found it was a Native American Medicine Wheel. This led him to study with elders of that land and eventually teach in his own way. He has written several books on the Medicine Way and teaches all over the place. All this arose from a simple inner journey. Try this and see what you discover.

Sit still and quiet and become focused within. Allow your breathing to slow, and give yourself permission to enter the deep realms and find a symbol, picture, feeling or guide which will lead you towards the path you will gain most from following.

Imagine clearly that you are standing in a deep and ancient forest, with all kinds of trees around you, and at your feet is a narrow path. The air is warm and you feel protected and at peace. You walk slowly along the path, feeling the breeze, smelling the leafmould, hearing the birds singing. Although it is dim under the leafy branches, you see ahead of you a wider clearing, where shafts of sunlight pierce the canopy and illumine the grass and wild flowers in the glade. As you get there you are at first dazzled by the light, but your sight clears and you look around. You discover that there are many paths leading off from the sunlit place into the gloom of the forest. One of those paths will take you towards a symbol which will be of greatest help at your present state of development. You must choose freely which way you will walk. If you sink deeper into relaxation, the direction will occur to you, absolute and certain, as if you had known it all the time. You walk that way, until the scenery changes. (Spend as long as you need, discovering what kind of symbol is there for you. Be patient and something will show itself to you.)

After a long while you know what form the symbol takes and you may be able to carry it with you or record every detail of it to know later on. Whether you know exactly what it is immediately or whether it is strange to you, remember it, and gently, mentally, retrace your steps to the sunlit glade. Linger there a moment or two, recalling all you can and then let the image gently dissolve. Feel yourself moving from that place to your own place, from that vision to the real world, and feel the blessing upon you as a gift from the Inner Worlds.

The thing you saw or discovered may need research to explain itself to you, but again, once you start to ask, skim through books and open your mind to a new and deeper awareness, you will find a clue and within about a month a path will be there for you to follow.

Exercise Twenty-two

Encountering an Archetype

This is another journey into the Wildwood, so allow yourself to become still, focused and able to sink into that altered state of mind in which true images and inner experiences may come to you.

Once again you are in the ancient Enchanted Forest, surrounded by many kinds of old, untouched trees. Below them there is little undergrowth and many narrow paths wander off into the distance. Again, trusting your inner senses, you choose a path and walk swiftly along it, winding through the forest. You notice how the path begins to climb and rocks break through the soft loam. The trees shrink in size, becoming twisted and dark, and clinging to ever steeper and rockier hillsides. Looking ahead, the way can be seen to clamber up an outcrop of pale rock and it is just possible to see the battlements of an ancient castle perched on the rock. This is a traditional stone castle, with round towers and pointed roofs with coloured banners flying from them.

You scramble up the steep path until it arrives at the entry to the castle. This is over a narrow stone bridge spanning a deep but waterless moat. There are no parapets either side, and you see how narrow and crumbly the bridge looks, yet you need to cross in order to enter. Take your time and know that you have the courage needed to cross such an insubstantial arch.

Swiftly and lightly you cross the stoney span and arrive at the castle gate of ancient wood. This too seems to block your way, but you cry out, 'Let me in, for I am on a great Quest,' and silently the door swings open. Beyond is a courtyard with many doors opening from it. Again you have to make a choice. Will you climb the steps to a great double door or enter a narrow arch, leading into darkness? There are always many options.

The way you choose leads you into a small and dimly lit room. As you start to see more clearly you make out a high barred window letting in sunlight. There is a table in the middle of the room made of huge thick oak planks. Behind it stands a robed figure. You need to decide which kind of help this might be. Is it the wizard Merlin, with his magical powers and special insights? Is it Morgan Le Fay, the sorceress and keeper of women's mysteries? Is it Arthur himself, the royal sovereign of the land, or is it Sir Kay, the guardian and protector of the sacred space? It could be any of these or even other archetypal beings who are here for you. Spend some time sitting across the table from the being, sharing a cup of spiced wine and learning from it. (Pause a while.) Eventually you notice the light is fading and it is time to depart. Give thanks to the person you have met there and say that you will return in the future to make another communication.

Slowly walk away from the room with the great table and find your way to the courtyard. From there you can swiftly pass through the gate and onto the narrow bridge. Somehow it feels wider and more solid. You see the path that leads through the Enchanted Forest safely and gently back to your home place.

Allow the images to fade and feel your own body. Stretch and take a few deep, slow breaths. Get up and stamp your feet. In order to feel fully at home, have a hot drink. While the kettle boils, jot down what you saw, whom you met, the shape of the great oak table and the things that were upon it. These are all important clues to your future.

Chapter Eight
Seeking Out Magical Roots

'Behold, we arise with the dawn of time from the grey
and misty sea, and with the dusk we sink into the western
ocean, and the lives of men are strung like pearls on the
thread of his spirit; and never in all his journeys goes he
alone...'

Dion Fortune, *The Sea Priestess*

Nearly everyone who takes a serious interest in magic seems to
have some 'far memories' of previous magical lives. As I have
said before, most magicians in the Western Mystery Tradition
and many modern witches accept reincarnation as a reality.
They may have been led through a variety of exercises which
allow them to recall past lives, or maybe scenes and experiences
from the past have bubbled to the surface of memory through
ordinary dreams and meditations. In some of the older schools
of magic, as well as having to search deeply into aspects of our
current lives as part of the 'Know Thyself' philosophy, it is
necessary to uncover who we may have been in the past.

Knowledge of our former selves can be both a blessing and a
bane, for we can add the failures of past lives to those of our
lives today or we can discover forgotten skills, knowledge and
power from the past. If you decide that there are things from
the past that you feel would help you to understand your position now, then there are a variety of ways of getting at the

memories, gently and completely. It is necessary, though, to be aware that delving into the far past will not help with the problems of today. It is not a definitive cure for all the ills of this life to blame current fears, failures and addictions on the lingering effects of past selves. Sometimes regression therapy can help discover the cause of certain phobias, some caused by events early in this incarnation and some left over from the lives before. But it is not a guaranteed cure of these fears nor is it a way of gaining confidence, for previously you can find yourself in a less favourable position than now.

Many witches today who accept the idea of reincarnation state that they recall being burned at the stake in a previous life. History, however, tells another tale. The punishment for witchcraft, in England, was hanging. Those burnt at the stake were accused of heresy. Many people did die in house fires, however, as the heating and lighting was flame, and the houses often of wood with a thatched roof. People died in floods, under fallen trees, of diseases which we readily survive now and women died in childbirth. Few in any century beyond our current one died in their beds of old age. Lots of men died in battles, and, though women still outlived their menfolk, they seldom had peaceful or healthy old ages. Life was tough and very few rose to the heights of fame or power or riches.

Dr Helen Wambach, throughout her life, led many thousands of people into past life recall through group hypnosis. She took these groups back to specific periods in history and due to the large numbers, she was able to show the statistical make up of European populations in the past. This data showed that about 90 per cent of people were peasants, slaves, serfs and ordinary common folk. A few were craftsmen and women, some were priests, and a tiny minority were nobility. Her researches, detailed in two books, *Reliving Past Lives* and *Dreams of the Future*, which takes hypnotic subjects into the future in a similar way, provide extensive evidence of the continuation of human existence.

Although I have not worked with groups, in the last 20 or so years I have led several hundreds of people in Britain back into the past using a variety of techniques. There are some methods which work like inner journeys and which can be used as doors to open the way to far-memory. These can work for individuals who are trying to remember the long ago lives, especially where they can recall scenes from the past. The scenes can often occur as the sense of *déjà vu* when you visit a place for the first time and know it as if you have been there before. You may find items in museums or old houses or castles scattered about the land which you visit while on holiday spark off a memory, or the feel of stately homes seems reminiscent. Even pictures on television can cause a feeling of familiarity or begin a quest for a long-lost memory.

The most effective way of remembering your past lives is through hypnosis. However, it really is important that you find a genuine and experienced hypnotist to help with the process rather than try to do it yourself. Although there are lots of people in Britain who practise hypnosis and a good many who offer either regression therapy or past life recall, not all that many have the magical background which is essential if you are to recover memories of rituals, healing methods or other esoteric material. Much ancient knowledge was gained under oaths of secrecy and though many hundreds, if not thousands, of years have gone by since those oaths were taken, they still have power, and can still the tongue and prevent memories from coming to light. If the hypnotist is a magician or initiate she will have ways of exploring those ideas, gently but firmly, so that ancient knowledge has a way back to the modern world.

Most of the important magicians of the past, particularly those whose books have been published in the second half of this century, had personal experiences of past life recall. Some had spontaneous memories brought about by visiting a traditionally sacred place, like Glastonbury or Stonehenge, others brought back recollections by meditation and others were guided to recover aspects of their earlier lives by their magical colleagues. Often these memories arise quite early in life and even children may recall parts of their last incarnation. This is very hard for them, because few adults, outside the esoteric world, understand that the tales of small children may be accurate memories of other lives rather than fantasy. When youngsters are brought up by understanding parents, however, they find their stories accepted.

Because it is essential to truly know yourself in all respects, the need to probe the memory for lost or forgotten knowledge is often a part of initiates' work. The Masters of lodges are not necessarily interested in their students being Napoleon or Cleopatra (though none I have met thought they were) but in their possible knowledge of things now forgotten.

According to esoteric philosophers, nothing that has ever been known is now lost forever. It may have been forgotten for thousands of years, but if someone who had that knowledge in a past life can be found and helped to recall it, then ancient wisdom may be retrieved. Lost ways of healing, magical arts and forms of divination have all been recovered by far memory and are used today.

Other kinds of information may also come to light during past life memories. The way the common folk lived and what they thought about, the way they conducted their own occupations and how they celebrated their religions outside the churches have been overlooked by the learned historians. For the most part the records deal with kings and bishops and armies, rather than the lives of the peasants and their daily grind. The simple country folk could not read or write, so few records of them are to be found in history books, yet they were the largest percentage of any population. Only by going back into the past is it possible to learn the details of humble folk, the poor, the serfs and the peasants. Each had a story as valid and interesting as that of the nobles or the priests. The country wisdom of living in harmony with the Earth, knowing the value of plants for food, for dyes, for healing and for magical processes, was in their hands, yet few traces of this store of knowledge are to be found in today's history books.

It is often asked how you can prove what someone is describing as a previous life is true. The short answer is that you can't, but as personal ways of trying out regression become more readily available, anyone can try it for themselves. What it feels like – and feelings have a valuable part to pay in esoteric knowledge – is that the memories are as real and have the same kind of impact when recalled as do memories of this life. When you remember what it was like to be in a battle, for example, it feels the same as recalling being in a car crash. Your reactions show the same degree of speeded pulse, anxiety and concern. Of course, many of the memories are pleasant and less traumatic. What is most strange is that you have an absolute certainty that what you are recalling is as genuine a memory as your first home. It does take a lot of patience, however, as memories are often remembered and described in 'real time', that is, they take as long to describe as they would have taken to happen.

It takes courage and trust on the part of the time traveller to venture into the past. It takes a similar degree of commitment to those who are guiding the traveller. It can take quite a long time, because getting into the right frame of mind, the right level of attentive relaxation, very like that used in meditation, requires practice. It also needs a quiet space in a day or evening, for once through the barrier, the traveller may wish to voyage for over an hour.

Using hypnosis may bring in further matters to think about. Nearly everyone can be hypnotized by someone, although this may require some research. Most people can allow themselves to drift into a sufficiently deep level to give them freedom to escape the here and now. What has to be accepted is that all hypnosis is *self-hypnosis*; though you may, as a subject, be taking note of what the hypnotist says, you are choosing to let her words affect you. You can always stop if you are not enjoying the process, or you can allow yourself to sink into deep relaxation and so awaken far memory. The hypnotist in recall sessions has to be very aware that her questions might cause the subject to react adversely. I heard one such case where the subject was describing an old life but the hypnotist asked her whether she could see any cars. This question had no meaning to her in her past experience, but it showed that you have to choose more oblique questions to ask. You can reasonably say, 'Are there any forms of transport around?' and the answer could be a car or a boat or a chariot. That is where the fascination for this aspect of modern magical psychology comes in. It really is extraordinary when a calm and relaxed person can start describing houses, towns, costumes and events from long ago.

You usually have to take the first trip of this sort on trust as it is impossible to judge where or when a person might go. In practice it is quite safe and your experience will be gentle, so long as you trust the people you are with. It is not a good idea to try this alone, although if dreams or meditations start to throw out material, you will have to deal with that on your own. Once you have found a way through the time barrier and relaxed enough to start seeing things, you will usually be able to describe the scenes to your companions. As you describe them, the scenes will become clearer and more real, until you feel you are actually there. Quiet questions from your guide will prompt you to say what you are wearing and what sort of place you are in. The more you are able to describe to your friends, the deeper you will be able to explore where you have landed. The really hard task is being able to ask a traveller the right sort of questions.

Many people are afraid that they will remember their last or previous deaths, and the kind of hypnotists who take people back through this life to birth and then back to the last life tend to allow this to happen. It is not a good idea, as it can be very frightening, especially if the subject is a man and finds himself dying in childbirth! By allowing travellers to drift gently back while in a relaxed frame of mind, it is possible to direct them to arrive on a 'good day', in a light place and in circumstances which feel comfortable. Once they have arrived, it may be your task to gently question them – and *gently* is the key word.

Travellers may well tell you what sort of landing they have

had, what they are wearing and the kind of surroundings they are in, but you can't always expect them to know where in geographical terms they are, nor what year it is. Often these factors have to be teased out from what is said, the description of the clothes or architecture. Travellers in foreign lands do not naturally speak Chinese or medieval French in answer to questions, because it is their modern mind and knowledge which is talking to you. Often they cannot immediately recall their names, which would seem an obvious thing to remember. Dr Helen Wambach, in her mass regressions, found she could ask travellers to 'flash' on these facts, seeing them as instant bits of knowledge, but it doesn't always work.

The questions need to be fairly general, for example, asking whether they are wearing shoes, rather than 'What kind of shoes are you wearing?' Most people were peasants and may not have had any shoes at all in the past. Ask if the traveller feels male or female. This may seem obvious, but it is common that people change sex during their strings of lives. Often the clothing and the kind of buildings can give you a clue about the country, the historical period and so on, but unless you are well versed in history, these clues may need later research. If you can guide your travelling friends through a pleasant day, you may gain information about food, markets, crops and crafts of the period, all of which can indicate location and perhaps time of year.

Always give the traveller plenty of time to answer. If travellers start to explain their situation spontaneously, let them get on with it, as questions might break their concentration and lessen the experience.

Gradually you will find a traveller's description becomes very vivid and if you are experienced, you can use it as the text of an inner journey, so that you can share some of the details of place and people with your friend. I have found that I can see clearly what the traveller is describing and often, afterwards, when we talk at length about what she saw and felt, I can show her the colour of the dress or draw a picture of the cart she saw, which I shared through psychic vision. Some of you who are clairvoyant may be able to do the same. It is helpful because if you see a building, for example, in the background of the vision, you can ask the traveller to go towards it and see it in detail. The way any building is made, what it is constructed of, and its size and position in relation to other buildings can be vital clues to follow up later.

If you do choose to explore the past yourself or share this experiment with friends, do be patient and gentle in the process. It can be quite scary, especially if the experience is very vivid and full of details. It can cause a kind of culture shock, because most people do not readily accept that reincarnation is true! To suddenly find yourself in a familiar but different body, in a place you have never seen before, can be a considerable surprise. I remember one fellow I took back who was quite unsure as to the possibility of many lives and the place he landed in was some sort of medieval building with a stone staircase. He did not move from that place nor explore any other visions. He could not even see his own feet or hands. What he did say afterwards was that he knew for an absolute fact that he had never seen that building in his current incarnation. From the point of view of an experiment it was very dull, but for George it was life-expanding. From the certainty that he would some day die came the new feeling that later on he would live again. It changed his whole outlook. If you try this, be prepared to see life and the world anew after the experience.

There are lots of ways of going about past life recall, and, as I said, although hypnosis is the fastest and most vivid experience which is available to many people, you do need an experienced hypnotist whom you trust. Trust is vital in all aspects of magical work and if you have the slightest quiver of doubt about anyone or any situation, give it a miss! There will always be a better chance later on. However, there are a number of techniques which anyone with a bit of common sense can use. As usual, you can use meditation, working on the theme 'Who am I now? Who have I been before?' You do need to work on both questions, one at a time, for a while. Of course, you need to be trusting of your own realizations with this process. No one will be there to ask questions, so each time you will need to prepare yourself by focusing on a particular idea or activity. It does take time, patience and inner effort, but if you are alone, then it may be the only way.

A way that is as safe and gentle as anything for a group of friends is to use an inner journey which takes you through time by passing through an imaginary 'time-tunnel', seen as an ordinary corridor with many doors leading off it. Each door represents a possible past age in which you may have lived. As you are instructed by the narrator to wander down this tunnel you will probably feel drawn to one or other of the doors. On the outside it might be quite plain and modern or its construction might represent the era it conceals. Try it from the exercise at the end of this chapter. You can do this with one or more friends, allowing time to move, float, walk or fly down the time-tunnel until each finds a door to open. Beyond it the experience may be individual and vivid or it might not work. When everyone has returned, after a suitable pause of about 10 to 15 minutes, ask them to write or draw their inner vision before all discuss their experiences. Each will have seen or felt things in an individual way, some more clearly than others, but it is a useful skill to master.

Another method which is in the public domain and so is safe for any group to try is a technique called the Christos Experience. It doesn't have any Christian overtones, it was simply called that when it was developed in America in the 1960s. There are several books on this by G. M. Glaskin, an Australian who made it popular at parties and in a very informal setting. You need a minimum of three people, but four is better, as there is a spare person to make the tea, answer the door or attend to any other disturbance. It takes about an hour in full, so do not rush off to some other activity without leaving plenty of time. To start with you need to decide who will travel, who will be in charge and who will keep a record, on audio tape, video or in writing. Other than recording equipment, there needs to be a place for the traveller to lie down flat with a pillow for her head, with room at each end for one of the others. In most of the sessions I have been involved with, the travellers lie flat on the floor or on sleeping bags with a low pillow for their heads.

The leader usually takes the head end and the recorder the feet, for the start of the process, which requires them to lightly massage their end of the traveller. The leader gently massages, with a firm circular motion, the area of the Third Eye, on the forehead above the bridge of the nose. It is usually easiest to do this with the ball of the thumb. The recorder or foot person gently massages the ankles and tops of the feet. Shoes, but not necessarily socks, need to be removed. With the traveller lying comfortably, with arms relaxed at the sides, the massage continues as described. The traveller should lie still and calm with her eyes closed and listen to what the leader has to say. This technique is not a hypnotic one and the traveller will be able to talk all the while. If she gets scared or bored or uncomfortable, she can simply open his eyes and sit up, ending the session. The leader should note any movements showing distress.

The leader instructs the traveller to feel herself stretching out through her head by about a hand's breadth. When the traveller says she can do this, the leader tells her to shrink back to her normal length. She is then told to imagine herself stretching out through her feet by the same sort of length and returning when she has done so. At each stage the traveller must confirm she is feeling or doing as she is asked. Then she should try to stretch through her head much further and return, then through her feet and return. Next she needs to stretch out at both ends until she feels she is floating upwards, out of her body. When she says she is doing this, both ends of massage should cease. Sometimes you can stop the massage quite early if the traveller is seeing clearly and feeling herself stretch.

Once she feels she has expanded and is floating, tell her she can float through ceilings and roofs until she is above the building. She can land there safely. From that vantage point allow her to describe what she can see. Reassure her she can't fall off and that she is quite safe. Ask her to look all around, seeing the place from that viewpoint. Next ask her to gently float to the ground and to describe in detail the front of the building she is in, its door, windows and garden, and so on. This all helps her get used to talking whilst travelling.

The next stage is to turn her vision of the familiar world from day to night by asking her to see the scene in darkness. When she has been able to do this successfully she will be ready for the next step, the move through time. She needs to be asked whether she really wants to go on, and of course, if she says no, then the process must be ended. If all is well, the leader tells the traveller to imagine herself floating up to rest on a soft white cloud. When she is there, she can be told that the cloud will be drifting through time, floating swiftly back through many years, until it arrives at a day and place where she was safe, content and living an interesting life. When she feels enough time has unravelled, she should be instructed to float to the ground gently, in daylight. Every question must be answered and she must always have plenty of time to allow the new pictures, feelings and so on to become clear. This basic process usually takes between 15 and 20 minutes in someone who has not tried it before. Those who are practised can get through it in a few minutes and the early exercises can be simplified.

Once the traveller has landed safely, you will need to ask her the same sorts of questions about what everything looks like, what she is wearing, and so on. This process may take about 45 minutes, but always allow the traveller plenty of space between questions to describe her activities, feelings and what she can see. After about three quarters of an hour, unless the traveller is having a great time (despite the fact that she is lying still, flat on her back and only moving her eyes), you can say, 'Are you ready to come back yet?' If she says yes, then she only needs to allow the pictures to fade and then she can open her eyes, sit up and drink the cup of tea the third member of the party has made! A hot drink will help her to return to her ordinary state of mind and be ready to answer all your questions.

It is a fascinating process and really does allow anyone to venture into the past, gently and securely, so long as she is able to trust their friends who share the experience. It can pose lots of questions about long-held theories of reincarnation, because the experience for most travellers is intriguing and real. A few people don't stray from the present time, but find themselves reliving a favourite holiday or visiting a special part of the world. These are usually the people who find it very hard to accept even the possibility of living more than once. Sometimes a second trip, a few weeks after the first, helps them to get over the mental barricades which prevent a deep experience. Trips of this sort must always be taken freely and not be forced on anyone, because there can be situations which frighten people, especially if they have had little or no experience of meditation or relaxation processes. This is not a game to be played by youngsters, either. Small children may indeed have strong memories of episodes from previous lives, but they should be allowed to let these fade until they are at least 16 years old. Then they will be able to cope with the adult knowledge and experiences safely.

None of these or any of the other ways of recalling far memories can prove reincarnation to be a fact. A large part of the world's faiths accept the idea, although the Eastern concept is very different. In some traditions the soul evolves through various animal forms before becoming human. In the West it is generally accepted that human souls have always been human in form, from their first creation. If you want proof, you will have to find a process which will allow you personal remembrances. It can only be known subjectively, yet there are thousands of people in Europe who have clear and distinct memories of past existences on Earth.

Some people are afraid of trying to find out about the past for they fear pain or death. From the work that I have done with hundreds of people over more than 20 years, I can assure you that memory of painful events does not present you with past agonies. Pain is a suffering of the body and that has been laid to rest at the end of that incarnation. Yes, you can recall dying, but it feels like a release, a freedom to enter the Realms of Light, the tunnel from death to afterlife, whatever faith you have lived. There can be other emotional responses too, of course, for you can recall old loves from long ago, the birth of children, the death of friends. You may recall turmoil and battles or peace and gentle existence in a simple rural idyll. You may find you can remember the way traditional festivals were celebrated or how old crafts were performed. Things seen in museums as 'cult objects' might be known to you and their use fully understood. You might gain confidence because in the past you overcame difficulties which plague you today and so you know you can overcome them. You might be able to fill in gaps in historians' knowledge about the long-lost past or you might bring back insights which take wisdom some long steps into the future. All these things are possible, but it may cost you the loss of some old long-held theories about life, the universe and everything.

There are questions still to be answered, but there is a vast literature on reincarnation memories and books on it have been published since the 1920s. There are books on experimental research, personal memories, historic and scientific studies and personal accounts. Many novels have been written as a result of far memory or based on other people's memories. Many writers today draw on long-forgotten ideas which come to them in visions and dreams. Some recall the future and their science fiction or fantasy works have future memories built in.

In order to decide whether you wish to explore your own past lives, it is worth spending a little time with a notebook, jotting down any dreams, experiences of *déjà vu*, feelings of 'homecoming' to strange places or any other tiny, insignificant fragments of memory which could be clues to some kind of past existence. If they seem high flown or unlikely, put those aside for the moment, but if any feel really important you can work on them. You might like to try the following exercise.

Clues to Recollection

To try this, which is another inner journey, you need plenty of time and a quiet setting. Sit down and relax and feel calm. Allow any scene from the past, be it from dream, visit of a new place or whatever, to arise in your inner vision. Feel the atmosphere creeping over you. Sink into the experience and allow it to fill your vision. Gradually you will start to notice changes occurring in the scene. There will be movement, a sense of air blowing perhaps, or a figure might enter the picture. Try to be ready to accept this without interfering or wishing to make alterations yourself. Simply watch and wait, and after a while you may find yourself in the scene, seeing it and experiencing what is happening. When this is well established, you will find that you can move the action on, or go to another place or time in that recollected life.

Allow yourself to explore for a little while the first time, later building up how long you can concentrate on each occasion. When you are ready to depart back to the here and now, just allow the scene to fade, go misty or darken and slowly bring yourself back to your starting-place.

This is not an easy exercise, it takes patience and thought. However, once you have made it work, you can explore further, all the time gaining control of the other self and its actions. Don't try too hard, nor too often. One such trip a week may well be enough, especially if you need to record your vision and perhaps research the historical details. Be careful – the changes you may experience in your views on the matter of life, death and reincarnation may be radically changed by this or any similar experiments.

Exercise Twenty-four

Entering the Time Tunnel

This is an exercise which really needs a minimum of three participants and a maximum of seven. One person needs to act as narrator and so should not attempt to travel in time. The narrator will have to watch all the others to see whether they are showing any signs of distress or fear. If you have a group of friends willing to try this, you can swap roles on different, well spaced out occasions.

Get everyone to sit down, become calm and still, and totally relax. These first parts of the journey are really important. If people keep on moving about they will upset the rest by the noises they make. If it takes five minutes for everyone to settle down and be relaxed, it is time well spent.

The narrator then says, 'You are walking down a wide flight of stairs, old polished wood with a soft carpet. It is very quiet and you feel calm and ready for an adventure through time. At the bottom of the stairs there is a long corridor with many doors leading from it. The lighting is soft and as you move along the corridor you are able to see that all the doors are different. Some may be coloured brightly or they may be old-fashioned wood with brass fittings. As you go along, there is one door which seem to draw your attention. Examine it so that you would recognize it again. Know that it might contain scenes from one of your previous lives. Take your time and when you are ready, see if you can open the door.'

At this point you should allow a minute of silence so that everyone can get to that point. Some people will do so easily, others may not succeed. Then say, 'You may gently open the door just a little so that you can see through to what is beyond. That place is quite safe for you to explore. Allow yourself to see that beyond the door is another scene, a place different from here and now. It is somewhere that you have lived in the past. The pictures will come clearer and you can safely step through the door.' Again pause for a short time.

Your next instruction is for anyone who has not managed to get to the door or see anything beyond it. Say, 'If you see only darkness or have no feeling of being in the corridor, allow yourself to relax and drift gently while the others explore their vision. As you relax, images or feelings may well drift into your mind, so just feel at ease.'

As several of your friends have managed to get through into the past, you can simply be quiet for about 15 minutes while they explore, or you can tell them to become aware of what they are wearing, any buildings near them and anything else visible to them. They don't have to speak, just remember to write down their experiences later on.

After a while, or if you notice any of the travellers getting restless, you need to gently bring them back. Say, 'The pictures before you are starting to become hazy and dim. They are merging into a rainbow-coloured mist and fading away. As you let them go, remember what you have seen or felt or experienced for later on. Gradually you become aware that you are standing outside a half-open door which is in a long corridor. See the door clearing and then firmly close it. You can walk swiftly along the passage, passing many other doors, and at the end you see a flight of wide stairs. You begin to climb the stairs, noting the soft carpet. Gradually you feel yourself returning to where you were to begin with. You feel safe and comfortable in your modern body, quite relaxed but full of interesting information. Gently open your eyes, feel your feet and clap your hands. Take a few deep breaths and wriggle about. When you are fully alert, get a notebook and pen and write down as much detail as you can remember. Take your time to jot down notes or make drawings. If you don't recall any pictures, note any feelings or ideas that may have occurred to you.'

Allow everyone plenty of time to make their notes before asking anything. At this time it is best to make a hot drink and find some biscuits for everyone. Once they have finished their writing and their snack, you can start to ask each individual about their experience. It is also a good idea to ask whether there were

any criticisms of what you said, as this will help in future exercises. There may be all sorts of reactions to the experience, so
take time to get everyone to feel alright about it. This kind of
exercise can be tried about once a week if you are beginners, but
of course more experienced people can alter it and use it as
often as they need.

When everyone has shared the experiences, you can decide
whether you want to start the historic research to back up their
discoveries or whether you will accept the exercise as a form of
mental training.

Chapter Nine
The Path of Initiation

'Child of Light, now wilt thou enter with us the Temenos
of the Adepti, wherein shall be undertaken the work of
the Portal; and this shall be to thee both a fulfilment of
the Lesser Mysteries and a preparation for the Greater...'

Melita Denning and Osborne Phillips,
The Foundations of High Magic

Many people who are drawn by the idea of magic seek initiation
and often feel that this would be the pinnacle of their training.
They are convinced that having undergone some ceremony of
initiation into a coven or lodge they will immediately have
immense power and knowledge, that all the problems which
beset them will be solved and a fortune is just round the corner.
Sadly, they will find this simply is not so. Initiation comes from
the Latin word *Ineo*, which means 'I go in'. It is an entry, not a
completion of the work. A first step, not adeptship, will be
offered at the conclusion of the rite and many years of hard
work and dedication will be needed to complete the training.

There are many different kinds of initiation on offer today,
but many of them require that those who wish to join that organization undergo at least a year of study. This is well worth
doing as it helps the would-be initiate learn the tradition of the
group and it allows those who are already initiates to get to

know the newcomer. These training courses vary in form. As already mentioned, some groups have what is called an 'Outer Court' where groups of students meet regularly to study different aspects of the group's work, from pagan festivals to the Qabalah. As the students work through the instruction, it is easy to see which of them is the most keen and dedicated. The same applies to groups which draw their members from a wider area, for they often offer preliminary teaching by correspondence. Again, the work done by individual students will be corrected and their abilities and motives clearly seen. This may not satisfy some people, especially if they are convinced they are already prepared for initiation and simply need to find the group to join.

Getting into a magical group or coven is supposed to be a bit of an effort, for those within have deserved their position. It is not like going along to evening classes or joining a flower growers' club. There will be commitment on both sides. From the newcomer there will be a sense of expectation and curiosity, and from the existing members there will be feelings of concern as to whether the newcomer will fit in and be worthy of what the group has to offer. If there has been, as there should be, an Outer Court to which the newcomer has been invited, she will not feel so much of an outsider. During the year or so of the Outer Court meetings the student will have met some of the established members of the group because some of them will probably have led the training sessions and guided students through the meditations and inner journeys. When a student is ready and her work is acceptable to the senior members of the group, whether it is ceremonial magic or witchcraft, the invitation to join the inner group, lodge or coven will be offered.

In some traditions the student has to ask for admission, while in others the decision to advance from novice to initiate has to be made by the senior members of the group. Often only one person's vote against the newcomer being admitted is enough to prevent initiation taking place. This will not be an arbitrary decision on the part of the senior member. All those who have advanced in any serious magical group will have developed their psychic senses and will be able clairvoyantly to see whether the student is ready in all respects. She may be well versed in theory of magical work and have written excellent papers on mythology, but if she is not really comfortable with ritual or finds it hard to visualize, she may not yet be ready for admission to the group. During the basic training sessions everyone will be doing all they can to help all students reach acceptable levels of understanding and practice, and they will get to know the newcomers and to like them, but magical groups are closer than families and all need to be in harmony before new energies are introduced to the group.

If you happen to fail some test for a lodge or coven, don't be down-hearted. It is a small step backwards which, if you are honest with yourself, might be a blessing in disguise. There is always a good reason for someone not being admitted, often because there is a better group just round the corner. Every bit of Outer Court training will be worthwhile and useful, and your increased knowledge will guide you to a more suitable group in due course. Failure is not such an evil concept. It is a great teacher, because it makes you look at what went wrong. When things go right there is no easy way to understand how it happened. If things don't go as planned, then, using your valuable meditative arts, you can discover the cause. Wrongs can lead to a greater right the next time.

Of course, not all groups offer training first. Sometimes you meet people at a festival or public conference and they recognize your potential for their coven. In this case the initiation ceremony can be undergone quite swiftly and the training happens on the job, as it were. Because many wiccan groups are more religious than magical, the rites of that Mystery religion are more suitable for newcomers. After all, you don't have to be a Christian initiate to go to church. Some covens work in the same manner as orthodox faiths, with regular meetings at weekends and major gatherings at the Eight Sabbaths, which mark their ritual year. In the seasonal rituals, the High Priest and High Priestess act out the lives of their Goddess and God, and the opening of the rite calls the power of the gods to inhabit their priest and priestess. The rest of the coven witness and share the enactment.

Some witch groups are more interested in magic and perform all sorts of spells within the coven circle. Although there is no historical evidence that witches gathered in covens before the writings of Gerald Gardner, there are lots of groups of witches nowadays. What they do and how they go about their religion is very varied, depending on the roots of the tradition they follow. Many covens have no handed down tradition except that which has been found in books. Some witches are self-initiated and that is just as valid as any other form of induction, if the communion with the Great Ones is made.

The whole point of any initiation is that the candidate is put in touch with the powers, gods or angels behind the system. Seldom does this happen as a great peak experience, but rather as the dawning of knowledge and understanding. The ritual may put the newcomer through a series of traditional steps, whether it is into High Magic or witchcraft. These help the candidate to enter the open and malleable frame of mind which will allow her to perceive the power of the tradition.

Most systems follow a similar pattern, showing they have common roots in medieval craft guilds. Candidates may be either put into a white robe, hence the name 'candidate', from the Latin word for white, or in some wiccan traditions they may be naked, or 'sky clad'. They are often blindfolded and sometimes have a rope tied around them by which they can be led. The first part of the ceremony will be some sort of challenge or questions which determine the individual's will to continue or her knowledge gained from previous training.

In that helpless state, the candidate is brought into the circle or lodge and may be made to kneel to take an oath of secrecy or which 'marries' her to the group. If the group has any sense it will ensure that the candidate is properly instructed and prepared, and is willing to swear the oath of allegiance. There may be methods of humiliation, cleansing or purification, by scourge, or with water or fire. There may be further questions. In many traditions the candidate is expected to take a magical name or motto. This may be given by the initiators or it might have been chosen by the individual. It ought to be a secret name, despite the fact that many occult magazine articles are signed by authors called Thoth Pan Bach or Artemis Kali Kwanyin! Magical names have great power and should not be bandied about in casual conversation or, more often, despite oaths to the contrary, details of the initiation rite discussed at length. Oaths do matter, they are serious and if you swear one you must keep to the principles of it.

You will find that most initiation ceremonies you read about (and there are endless books which give details), also instruct the candidate about the symbols of the tradition, its gods or the use of the tools. It is a pity that students can read initiation scripts, because it gives them a false idea of what the experience is like. Certainly most groups, even those whose tradition is entirely derived from published sources, like much of modern wicca and groups working the Golden Dawn system, will actually rewrite the words or actions. Unless you are told to read such material before the event, it is far more valuable an experience if you know only a few details of the ceremony. If you are trying to remember what will be said next or when the blindfold will be removed and so on, you will miss the experience of hearing the words in darkness or of returning to light after darkness. These aspects of the ritual allow its magic, which, after all, is a willed change of consciousness, to occur.

There may be explanations during the ritual, and you may be introduced to your new brothers and sisters by their magical names, so it helps if you are fully concentrated upon what is said. Often this instruction is never given again and clues missed on the first occasion could be very important in the future.

After the main part of the ceremony, when you can see and move about freely, there is usually a communion meal and drink. This occurs in most rituals and is much older in form than the Christian communion. In the ancient Greek temples, rites were ended with the Agape, a love feast, which symbolized, among other things, the unity and brotherhood of the initiates. This is still the case, for sharing a cup or wine, fruit juice or spring water links all companions, not only with their living co-members, but with all initiates of that tradition and those who have died or who inspired their work.

Often there will be a real feast after the ritual when the new member is taken into the hearts of the others and the new-comer can formally meet the rest of the group. Becoming an initiate is a privilege, a rare honour, even in these days of wider information on the occult. The percentage of the population who are genuine initiates is about the same as it ever has been; there are very few dedicated magicians and witches. Lots of folk may claim to be initiates or witches or lodge members, but unless the connection has been made between the candidate and the gods of the system and there has been a two-way recognition, what they say is just hot air. If you find your way into the Mysteries, remember it is a very special commitment.

Initiation has two sides. One is that the novice has access to secret information and the power that such knowledge may bring. The second side is that of responsibility. The payment for hidden knowledge – and nothing in magic is free – is that you become a servant of Light. You learn in order to serve the cause of evolution. Magical power, inner names and ritual arts are not things you do in order to boast about them, for that is the fastest way to negate your power and destroy the bonds of friendship in any magical group. You are responsible for what you know, and it is best to take on secret knowledge with spiritually clean hands and an honest heart. You are responsible for making safe and sensible use of what you learn. The path of initiation is a school for those who need in-depth instruction, but it is also a path of service to humanity and it is never an easy option.

In some ceremonies of initiation there is an enactment of death and rebirth. The initiate is a new person, has a new horoscope and this is why she also takes a new name. Because of this ritual rebirth the novice can begin a new pattern of life, setting aside any parts of her previous existence. Although it may seem like amateur dramatics, a bit of a giggle even, it will still have long-lasting and perhaps transforming effects. Initiation, entered into seriously, whether experienced alone or as entry into a group, will alter the initiate's path in life. The changes may take time to become apparent and they may not seem to be linked to magic, but gradually the way the initiate perceives the world, the way she feels about things and reacts to situations, will alter. What she will have gained through initiation is like another dimension of experience or a further sense which will work in magical situations and will also be of use in everyday events.

Most forms of magical training will have more than one level. Witchcraft in covens has three degrees, borrowed by Gerald Gardner from Freemasonry and the practical guilds that went before. In High Magic there may be many degrees – the Hermetic Order of the Golden Dawn has ten, but living humans can really only receive some of these – and other sorts of magical and spiritual traditions have a variety of grades and titles. The Druids, for example, have grades of Bard, Ovate and finally Druid. Degrees, like academic degrees, have to be earned, and are granted only when the student has achieved the knowledge and skill of the degree. Again, these are not things to boast about. Many of the higher degrees in most systems are guarded by further oaths of silence or discretion, so if you hear of people boasting that they are fourth degree witches or Ipssissimi in the Golden Dawn, judge them as human beings, rather than as exalted adepts.

Passing through grades or levels of magical power is a slow business and you can expect to take at least a year for most studies to earn the next rise of status. It is not a matter of simply learning certain things by heart, but of mastering the physical, spiritual and magical aspects of each Element, or the poetic arts. Each rise up the ladder brings further responsibilities. If you become a healer, then you must be able to heal; if your grade indicates you are a diviner, you must be able to read the Tarot accurately on all levels, not just know what the pictures mean. In well established groups the students rise as far and as fast as they are able, for magic is a meritocracy – if you can do it, then you can earn the praise. Every bit of learning has its value and within the circle all are equal, although their tasks may differ. So long as you are willing to continue with the everyday exercises and use them to explore new skills, you can continue to rise towards adepthood.

Ritual is an important part of much magic, but, as we have already seen, its value and use have to be understood. Simply copying a rite from a book without understanding the symbolism, words of power and intent will not help you. There are many spell books available and the spells in them will probably have worked for the person who wrote them, but that is not necessarily the author of the book. Since the Middle Ages, rituals, spells and charms have been copied and altered, re-written and handed down. Along that line of magic some of the writers have not tried out the spells or test-driven the rituals or other exercises. There are a great number of books written by people who have had no experience of actual magic. This is sad because if you try their rituals today and they fail to work, you will not be able to judge whether it was your fault or the fault of the ritual you copied.

This doesn't apply only to High Magic but to witchcraft and wicca too. If you are willing to trace the ideas given in various writings you may well find they either go back to a medieval source or vanish into thin air. People in the last half of the twentieth century who are so used to seeing information in writing, whether on a page or on a computer monitor, have forgotten that facts need to be checked. It is easy to pick up a new book by a seemingly learned author, enjoy the writing and perhaps feel that the information presented there, because it is in a book, must be true. Sadly this is becoming more common. Whole theories are being presented as fact, based on very flimsy research or pure speculation, and the students of today, not having the years of study behind them, do not have the knowledge to be able to check what is said.

If you are following a tradition, ask whether it is old or whether it has been reinterpreted by its modern practitioners. It is a simple question and may still need further meditation or reading to check. If someone did invent it last year, or, say, it is a reinterpretation, that doesn't mean it can't work, only that you need to be careful because its theory may not line up with what you know from other sources. If you want to take the time and trouble to look at the background it will be well worth it. Certainly a lot of modern magic is fairly new or at least may have been rewritten to suit the philosophy and life-styles of modern people. We are not all able to read Hebrew, Greek, Latin and Enochian, or even Old English or medieval French. These were the languages in which the earliest magical texts were written. Just as with the Bible, which was written in Hebrew and Aramaic, not modern English, meanings and interpretations have varied through time.

Magical rituals written by modern initiates, whether of ceremonial magic, Druidry or wicca, will work so long as the writer really knew what to do. However, no ritual will work unless its principles are thoroughly understood. You must know what god names mean and what sort of deity is being called upon for help. You must then recognize whether the symbols, colours, incenses and so on are appropriate. You must be especially sure that whatever power you are calling upon will be helpful, not harmful. If you don't know, then work out something different which you are certain will be safe.

Nearly all rituals follow a pattern. They require that a sphere of quiet and protection is set up; they generally call upon great beings of the quarters of heaven attend to empower, guard and support the work. The inner temple has to be built in the minds of all the participants, a temple appropriate to the work in hand, and it has to be maintained by shared effort during the ritual. There needs to be a clearly stated purpose which all concur with and time must be given to meditation to see that the purpose is just. All kinds of real work can be done in the heart of the ritual, when the expert diviner or healer has something to do, and there is usually a communion with all living beings towards the end of the ritual. The closing must be thorough and complete, and any remaining energy safely directed to a good cause. These steps may seem simple and brief, yet when you understand each of them they have enormous power and will be truly effective.

Initiations have the same sorts of pattern, although the candidate may not be present for the opening of the temple or circle of witches. If you are offered initiation, be very sure you really want it, into that group, now. There is no blame in deciding you are not happy with the coven or really can't get along with the High Priest or other members, or that you are not ready yet for the big and irrevocable step. Initiation is forever. You may be able to leave the group if you are not happy or if you grow out of their teachings, but once you have taken the ritual of initiation, on your own just as much as within a group, you are going to be an initiate forever. The promises of silence and discretion last for many lives and the commitment to do good, to heal, to take responsibility to care for the Mysteries, will call you back, life after life, once the initiation has been taken. Certainly it will also grant you companionship and access to knowledge which can lead to personal power and it will change your life, for your ritual death and rebirth will give you a new start, almost a new way of seeing the world, and a new name.

Before you commit yourself to any group there is a basic ritual you can do on your own, or with a few friends, which will help you to find the best path, alone or with some kind of school. It will give you a feel of ritual if you follow the instructions and do it sincerely. The results may not be immediate, as they often take time to come into being, but your efforts can lead you exactly to the path your soul yearns to follow.

Exercise Twenty-five

Seeking the Path to Everyday Magic

It is important to prepare fully for any ritual, but if you have not had much previous experience or this is your first ritual, please follow these instructions carefully and fully. You can't make a mistake in any rite if you are doing your best, but preparation can save moments of doubt and confusion later. It is necessary to collect certain items for ritual use, to find a time and place where you can be quiet and focused for at least an hour. To give power to the ritual you will need to meditate on your intention and call for magical force to flow in your working. To perform the ritual you will need to make a talisman of clean stiff white paper or thin card, with words written in black ink. You would also benefit by making your own ritual rubric, which is a hand-written text of the ritual, with the words to be spoken in clear black and the instructions and 'stage directions' in red. This will help you concentrate on the whole ritual and be fully aware of what has to be done and what is needed. There is also time at that stage, if you are more experienced, to make additions or changes to suit your previous instruction. To make the talisman which will represent the intent of the ritual, you need a small square of white paper on one side of which you write YOUR FULL NAMES and ANY NICKNAMES, the TIME AND DATE OF BIRTH and THE PLACE WHERE YOU WERE BORN or, if you feel you are really a citizen of somewhere else, that place. (This is to identify only you of the whole population of the world of people.) You can also link it with yourself by fixing some of your hair or blood or spittle, or carry it around with you for a few days.

You will need to prepare an altar table, as in the earlier exercise, together with two new candles. These can be both white or one white and one black (or very dark grey or brown). They represent the light of day and darkness of night, because once on your magical path you do not step off it by day or night. You will need matches of course to light the candles and if you are using incense with charcoal or joss sticks these should be of a single scent. Incense of frankincense or sandalwood, or joss sticks scented with rose or jasmine are best as they are gentle but uplifting. You could use a scented flower, a rose or carnation, for example, if you have them. You will need a chalice or goblet of either spring water or fruit juice (apple or grape are best) and a small plate with a piece of bread on it. There should also be rock or some earth from somewhere special to you. (Bought crystals are no use to this ritual, so go and find a stone or a handful of earth from a garden near you.) The earth or stone should be placed in a small dish or bowl. If possible this should be made of dark-coloured pottery or wood. You will see that all Four Elements are represented by these objects – Earth by stone/earth; Water by the goblet of spring water or juice; Fire of heaven and earth by the two candles; and Air by the scent of incense or the flower. The bowl with the earth and the plate with the bread both represent the circles of eternity and the power of Spirit, the fifth element within the ritual. You will also need an envelope which is big enough to take your talisman when it is folded in half and a black pen to write your intent upon the back of the talisman during the ritual. You will see that the words are in the ritual text, so be sure you understand them before you begin. You may prefer to use words of your own here, but they should have the same sort of implications.

If you have a robe you can wear it for this rite, otherwise wear clean and comfortable clothes of white or a pale colour, as you represent the candidate. If you have a cord to wear round your middle, you can use this to represent your entry into the Mysteries. There are old-fashioned kinds of cords used for dressing gowns or as curtain tiebacks which usually come in all sorts of colours and have tassels on the ends. Even if you are only going to wear everyday clothes or even do the ritual naked, a cord should still be used.

To begin, with, when you have copied the ritual (or better still, learned it by heart) and have made your talisman, you can lay out the altar. You will need to place the clean white cloth on it and then arrange the two candlesticks, white on the right and black on the left, as they represent the twin pillars of the temple, and the other items in front of them. Because this is a real ritual it is important to be able to walk around the altar if possible, because by so doing, you are marking out the sacred and special space within your room. If you simply don't have room to make a circle (and the ritual could be done out of doors if necessary), you will still need to be able to turn round in front of your chair, to address your words to the four directions.

When you are ready to begin, sit down and feel calm and focused on what you are doing. It is at this stage that you can still change your mind and give up or decide to try again on another occasion.

When you are satisfied, pick up your symbol of Earth, be it a stone or some earth, hold it at eye level and say, 'POWER OF EARTH, BRING STABILITY TO MY WORK.' Walk round the altar clockwise and when you get back to your seat, hold up the symbol and say, 'THE POWER OF EARTH IS PRESENT IN MY CIRCLE.'

Next pick up the goblet of water and say, 'POWER OF WATER, BRING DEEP FEELING TO MY WORK.' Carry it around clockwise and then say, 'THE POWER OF WATER IS PRESENT IN MY CIRCLE.'

Next strike a match and light the black then white candle. When they are lit put the matches aside. Pick up the white candle, raise it to eye level and say, 'POWER OF FIRE, BRING BRIGHT ENERGY TO MY WORK.' Carefully carry the candle around clockwise, then say 'THE POWER OF FIRE IS PRESENT IN MY CIRCLE.'

Again take the matches and light your joss stick (or, if you are using charcoal and incense, light the charcoal before you begin the ritual), then say, 'POWER OF AIR, BRING UNDER-STANDING TO MY WORK.' Carry the scent of incense of a flower round your circle clockwise, and at the end say, 'THE POWER OF AIR IS PRESENT IN MY CIRCLE.'

Finally, raise up the black candle and say, 'MAY THE

POWER OF THE SPIRIT AWAKEN MY POWER WITHIN ME FROM THE HEIGHTS TO THE DEPTHS. MAY MY CIRCLE PROTECT AND ENCOURAGE ME THROUGH-OUT THIS WORKING.'

Now sit down and see the energy flowing around the circle, outwards from the candles and brightly around all the things in front of you. Feel when you are ready to go on.

When you are content, pick up your pen and write clearly on the back of your talisman the words 'I SEEK TO FIND THE RIGHT PATH FOR ME IN EVERYDAY MAGIC.' Fold it in half and put it in the envelope.

You then need to bless the talisman with Earth, Water, Fire and Air and Spiritual Power. Do this by touching the envelope with the stone, then sprinkle a drop of water on it, then sweep it carefully above the white candle's flame, then through the incense or smell of the flower. Place it back on the altar in the middle and say, 'MAY THE POWERS OF THE ELEMENTS CLEAN, BLESS AND DEDICATE THIS TALISMAN TO HELP ME ON MY MAGICAL PATH.'

Sit down and meditate on what you have done and even at this stage an idea or helpful thought might creep in to your mind about your future.

Next take the cord and tie it round you, then say, 'I FREELY BIND MYSELF TO THE PATH THAT LEADS TO THE LIGHT. SO MAY THIS BE.'

After that pick up a piece of bread, hold it within the sacred light around the candles and say, 'BLESS THIS BREAD OF EARTH THAT IT MAY FEED MY SOUL.' Then eat it.

Take the goblet of water, hold it in the light of the candles and say, 'BLESS THIS WINE OF THE SPIRIT THAT IT MAY AWAKEN MY SOUL.'

Once again sit still for a few moments, feeling the atmos-phere and any energies moving around you. If you are clairvoy-ant, you may well see flowing lines and clouds of light about the room and your altar.

After a pause it is important to close down. You begin by

snuffing out the black candle and then say, 'THE POWER OF THE SPIRIT DEPARTS FROM THIS CIRCLE, BUT NOT FROM MY LIFE.'

Next you raise up the scented flower of incense, walk anti-clockwise round the altar, then say, 'THE POWER OF AIR DEPARTS FROM THIS CIRCLE, BUT NOT FROM MY LIFE.'

Pick up the white candle, carry it anticlockwise round the room back to its place and snuff it out, then say, 'THE POWER OF FIRE DEPARTS FROM THIS CIRCLE, BUT NOT FROM MY LIFE.'

Next carry the water goblet round anticlockwise and say, 'THE POWER OF WATER DEPARTS FROM THIS CIRCLE BUT NOT FROM MY LIFE.'

Finally do the same with the Earth symbol and say, 'THE POWER OF EARTH DEPARTS FROM THIS CIRCLE YET IT WILL ALWAYS SUPPORT ME AND SUSTAIN MY LIFE.'

Try to feel flows of energy seeping away until there is stillness and complete quiet around you. Write down what you have done and as you clear up, take the talisman in its envelope and put it under your bed or on top of a wardrobe, out of the way, until it has had time to work. This could be anything from a few days to a month or two. What matters is how much effort you put in by searching for guidance for yourself.

If there are several of you sharing this ritual, you will have to allocate the parts. It is usual to have different people carrying round the symbols of the Elements, for example, or blessing the drink and bread before passing it round.

Although this ritual has been designed for the purpose of making a talisman to help find a personal path to magic, the beginning and end can be used for other kinds of working, like healing or divination. If you know how to do that, then feel free to adapt this rite, but if you don't yet have that much experience, leave it until you do. The ritual as it is written is based on one that has been successfully worked by many people.

End Word

Anyone can have the power of everyday magic, but it will cost everyday effort and continual practice. We are all born with the potential to do many things – to work magic, to heal, to see into the future or to offer psychic help to others. Each of these skills is there to be learned, to be mastered by any individual, old or young, learned or less intellectual, rich or poor. Each of us inherits the seeds of this ancient wisdom, but we have to walk the paths of magic and make dreams come into reality.

Some students learn very fast, for in many previous lives they have gained powers and abilities which they quickly recall when they find the inner way in this life. If they enter any of the schools of occult knowledge they will all start at the bottom, but those with obvious talents in this direction will rise quickly through the ranks to regain their lofty status.

The doors to esoteric knowledge are open to all, but they have to be found. There are plenty of clues to be found in the hundreds of small magical, occult and wiccan magazines which are published in every land. These offer the signposts to students, from which a wide variety of roads can lead forth. To find the best one for you, the unique and wonderful person that you are, will require you to make an effort. I can't say become a witch, join the Order of the Golden Dawn, take up Druidry or seek out ancient wisdom from Egypt or India. All I can say is that there are many exciting paths to explore. All are safe if your heart is pure and your intentions honest. Use your common sense, develop your psychic powers, your abilities to see through time and space, and employ these as you reach forward. The Great Gods are all round you but invisible, and your Holy Guardian Angel hovers at your shoulder. The ways to wonder are all about you and the keys to saving the world may be in your hands. Seek and indeed you shall find, for there are blessings to be gained from everyday magic.

Bristol, June 1994

Marian Green would be happy to receive letters from anyone who is trying out the exercises in this book and will reply, time permitting, if return postage or International Reply Coupons are enclosed.

Book List

There are many excellent books written by practitioners of their arts. These are just a few of them. Most authors have written many other titles.

Butler, W. E., *Magic and the Magician*, The Aquarian Press, London, 1991

Denning, Melita, and Phillips, Osborne, *Planetary Magic*, Llewellyn, USA, 1988

–, *The Foundations of High Magic*, Llewellyn, USA, 1989

Fortune, Dion, *Applied Magic* and *Aspects of Occultism*, Aquarian, London, 1995

–, *Sane Occultism* The Aquarian Press, Wellingborough, 1967; now out of print

Franz, Marie Louise von, *On Dreams and Death*, Shambhala Publications, 1987

Glaskin, G. L., *A Door to Infinity*, Prism, Bridport, Dorset, 1989

Green, Marian, *The Path through the Labyrinth*, Thoth Publications, Loughborough, 1993

–, *A Witch Alone*, Aquarian, London, 1991

–, *Practical Techniques of Modern Magic,* Thoth Publications, Loughborough, 1994

Hope, Murry, *The Psychology of Ritual*, Element Books, Shaftesbury, 1988

Knight, Gareth, *Secret Tradition in Arthurian Legend*, The Aquarian Press, Wellingborough, 1983; now out of print

Leland, Charles, *Aradia*, Phoenix Publishing, Arizona, 1994

Matthews, John & Caitlin, *The Western Way*, Arkana, London, 1985; Penguin, 1994

Mayo, Jeff, *Teach Yourself Astrology*, Teach Yourself Books, English University Press, London, 1961; reissued Hodder, 1981

Ozaniec, Naomi, *Daughter of the Goddess*, Aquarian, London, 1993

Regardie, Israel, *The Golden Dawn*, Llewellyn, USA, 1940

Shân, *Circlework*, published by House of the Goddess, 33 Oldridge Road, London SW12 8PN, who also run training classes

Silva, José, *The Silva Mind Control of Mental Dynamics*, Granada, London, 1980; reissued Grafton Books, 1990

Stewart, R. J., *Advanced Magical Arts*, Element Books, Shaftesbury, 1988

Wambach, Helen, *Reliving Past Lives*, Arrow Books, London, 1980; now out of print

–, *Dreams of the Future*, Aquarian, London, 1991

Willis, Tony, *Magick and the Tarot*, The Aquarian Press, Wellingborough, 1988

–, *Discover the Runes*, Aquarian, London, 1991

Useful Addresses

There are literally hundreds of small magazines in the world which list groups, training courses, orders, covens and individual tuition. Read the articles in them, study the small advertisements and use your intuition to find clues. Send a stamped addressed envelope or an International Reply Coupon from any large post office world-wide, for current information. (These are small magazines and their addresses may change.)

BRITISH PUBLICATIONS

The Cauldron, Write to Mike Howard, Caemorgan Cottage, Caemorgan Road, Cardigan, Dyfed SA43 1QU.
Dalriada, 2 Brathwic Place, Brodick, Isle of Arran, KA27 8BN. (Celtic paganism.)
Kindred Spirit, Foxhole, Dartington, Totnes, Devon TQ9 6EB. (Available from large newsagents and New Age shops.)
The Occult Observer, Atlantis Bookshop, 49A Museum Street, London WC1A 1LY.
Pagan Dawn: Journal of the Pagan Federation, The Pagan Federation, BM 7097, London WC1N 3XX.
Quest, BCM SCL QUEST, London WC1N 3XX. (I edit this magazine.)
Talking Stick, PO Box 3719, London SW17 8XT.

WORLD-WIDE PUBLICATIONS

Circle Network News, PO Box 219, Mount Horeb, WI 53572, USA. (This publication issues an annual *Directory of Groups/Schools/Shops*.)

Diipetes, PO Box 20037, GR-11810, Athens, Greece. (In Greek.)

Isian News, Fellowship of Isis, Clonegal Castle, Enniscorthy, Ireland. (The Fellowship has groups all over the world and offers training.)

Magic Pentacle, Box 56–065, Dominion Road Post Office, Mount Eden, Auckland 3, New Zealand.

Wiccan Rede, PO Box 473, Zeist, NL 3700 AL, The Netherlands. (In Dutch and English.)

There are many more publications but each of these named above list other publications or are able to offer training or group gatherings themselves. Some also publish directories of groups, shops and training courses.